CW00665319

Prai

Kevin and ... .

"Relentlessly honest, refreshingly uncontrived, this diary really works. It has a "rough and ready" unpolished pizzazz and energy that make it a lot of fun to read."
- The Armchair Traveller, *Sunday Tribune*

"India, at low-budget tourist level, is buffeting and bullying. But over four months travelling, Frank Kusy remains indefatigably and irrepressibly jocular. More assault course than holiday, this reads so true that most of us will be grateful not to have to go there ourselves."
- Monty Haltrecht, *The Mail on Sunday*

"Easy to read, interesting and funny, you feel you are there with Frank and Kevin, cooped up in trains, starving for days and then going on massive binges, going thirsty and then drinking coffee, only to find that it's been sweetened with baboon's milk."
- Julian Cole, *The Mercury*

"An enjoyable travel tale that reads as if the author were in the room recounting stories from his holiday. Good pace, right amount of humour, and an interesting take on a fascinating country."
- Scott Pack, *Harper Collins*

"Vivid, hilarious and, at times, heartbreaking. Just like India. This is great travel-writing. Melts the plain vanilla past the evaporation point."
- Greg Levin, author, *Notes on an Orange Burial*

"Hilarious and absolutely brilliant! Move over Bill Bryson. This is where it's at!."
- Sarah Monaghan, author, *First Term at St Twitters*

Kevin and I
in India

Frank Kusy

First published in Great Britain 1986
by Impact Books, 112 Bolingbroke Grove,
London SW11 1DA

Reprinted 1990, 1995

Current edition published in 2013 by
Grinning Bandit Books
http://grinningbandit.webnode.com

ISBN 978-0-9575851-3-3

Cover design by Amygdaladesign

DEDICATION

To my mother and the Gohonzon

Foreword

Hi dear reader,

I find it hard to believe myself, but almost 30 years have passed since I first wrote 'Kevin and I in India'. It was my very first published book – a year or so before I was commissioned to write a series of travel guides to Asia – so I was both surprised and amazed when it won plaudits from such big international press names like the Sunday Tribune and the Mail on Sunday. I was even more amazed when it became an instant bestseller and ran three editions in paperback.

Last year (2013), after publishing a more recent book of my Indian adventures (called 'Rupee Millionaires'), I decided to re-release 'Kevin and I' as an e-book, but was plagued with doubts. 'Is it still worth putting out there?' I thought to myself. 'Is it still relevant to our times?' Well, the answer to both questions – thanks to a flood of lovely reviews on Amazon – was a resounding "Yes". India hasn't changed much, especially at backpacker level, and people who have never been to this wonderful country, and even those who have, are still enjoying our little 'diary of disaster' as we haplessly flung ourselves into three months of fun and self-imposed torture.

So why did we do it? Why did we expose ourselves to the most down and dirty (and yet often hilarious) time of our lives? Well, we really had no choice. We couldn't afford luxury hotels or comfortable transport or what few Western-style restaurants there were back then. All that we could afford was to tour India like Gandhi – living in the most basic of accommodations, travelling 3rd class by bus and train, experiencing this vital, funny, sad, curious, welcoming and altogether mind-blowing country at grass roots level. Would we do it again? Probably not. Were we glad we did it at all? We wouldn't have missed it for worlds.

Oh, and if you get to the end of this book, and are wondering what happened to Kevin, well, he is alive and well and living in Lowestoft. Every Christmas I travel up to see him, and we share the plate of cheese sandwiches that we couldn't find in India, and we look back and say to each other: 'Did we really do all that half a lifetime ago?'

Well, yes, we did.

Contents

Map

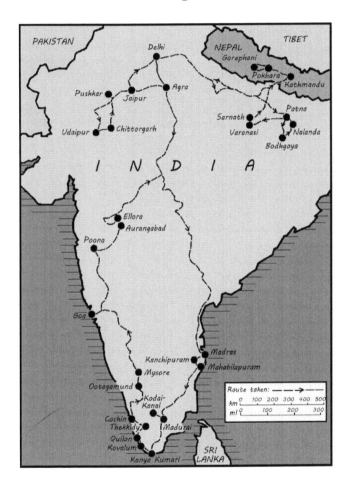

Epigraph

Ever thought how cool it must have been, backpacking
round India in the Eighties?

Well, think again...

x

Part One

Napoleon and the Deep South

January 3rd 1985

It was a cold, foggy morning when we landed. I was welcomed into Delhi by a flint-eyed Indian 'businessman', lying in wait just outside the airport. He wanted to buy my duty-free cigarettes and whisky. He was followed by six other traders, all wearing the same conspiratorial grins and all wanting exactly the same thing. The incredible prices they were offering sent my eyebrows soaring. I had just been introduced – during my first few minutes on Indian soil – to the country's thriving black market.

On the airport bus into New Delhi, I met up again with Kevin – the only other Englishman I had seen on my flight. I found him staring out of the bus window at the busy traffic thoroughfare beyond the airport concourse. Suddenly plucked from his sleepy bedsit in Lowestoft and set down on manic Mars, his square, ruddy face wore a look of open-mouthed astonishment. The traffic resembled a stock car rally, with every driver on the road blindfolded.

Everywhere we looked, buses, coaches, auto-rickshaws, taxis and huge public carriers were hurtling down the highway, cutting each other up with total disregard for their (or anyone else's) safety. There were indeed so many vehicles passing each other on the wrong side of the road that it was almost impossible for us to guess what the *right* side of the road was.

1

Kevin's sense of order and propriety was grievously offended. He hopped off the bus to see what would happen if he tried crossing the road on a nearby zebra crossing. All that happened was that he nearly got run over.

Peering through my round Lennon spectacles, running a contemplative finger over my bearded lips, I wondered what Kevin was *doing* here. Me, I'd come looking for the 'spiritual' India – I had taken up Buddhism recently and wanted to know where it all started. Kevin had no such excuse. If it was a holiday he was after – watching him so rashly dice with death – I didn't think he'd be getting one.

Teeth gritted, I took in the scene. Every vehicle, large or small, seemed to have a loud horn. And it weaved recklessly in and out of the speeding traffic, blowing its horn again and again. It was apparently the only way it expected to ever get anywhere. The collective effect of all these bus air-horns, car bleepers, rickshaw hooters and bicycle bells screeching and blaring away in competition with each other was absolutely deafening.

Our bus plunged into this chaos without warning. Two passengers having a quiet smoke outside were left behind. A couple of minutes up the road, the driver figured he'd missed a turning somewhere and ground the bus to a halt in the middle of the frantic traffic. Then he *reversed* it slowly back up the highway, leaning out of his window in search of the lost turning. The Red Sea of speeding vehicles bearing down on us from behind magically parted to permit this terrifying manoeuvre. One auto-rickshaw came so close, I could smell the wheels burning. Its tyres, I noted with astonishment, were not only bald. but the rubber was flapping away in loose strips along the hubcaps.

Kevin calmed his nerves by taking photographs. He managed to take a whole roll of film in just an hour. Mind you, there was a great deal to see: every few seconds we were getting tantalising glimpses of Indian life wholly unfamiliar to our jaded Western eye. Bullocks and camels strolled past, indolent and slow, impervious to the noise of the traffic. Old men and beggars were selling roasted nuts and holy blessings on the pavement. Large families of destitutes were lighting smouldering fires beside open sewers. Ragged women were scraping around in the filth and offal of the gutters for food for the next meal. Cripples and starving children lay helpless on the side of the road, empty-eyed and listless in their despair. Everywhere we looked, people were living on the bottom, bottom line. After a while, Kevin put away the camera.

Despite both coming to India alone, Kevin and I decided to take a room together this first night, at the YMCA hostel in Jai Singh Road. Little did we know it, but this was the start of a great adventure – we would be travelling together for the next two months, and covering the whole length and breadth of India.

It made sense to share accommodation in Delhi, which could be pretty pricey by Indian standards. Our double room cost us Rs135 (£10), but the Y's facilities for guests were superb. They included two resident travel agencies, where I was able to book a bus tour of Delhi, a traditional dance entertainment for a couple of days ahead, a three-day tour of Rajasthan, and finally, a first-class train berth for Madras for the following week. The latter arrangement was a huge relief. I had heard that queuing up for train reservations in Delhi station itself was the nearest thing to purgatory for the foreign tourist.

The hostel also had a useful currency-exchange desk in the reception area. This saved guests another supposedly awful ordeal: having to change money in regular Indian banks.

3

When, however, I appeared at this desk to make my first purchase of Indian rupees, it was deserted. But just outside the hostel entrance my problem was solved. A horde of unemployed rickshaw drivers rushed up, all wanting to buy my cash dollars on the black market. The exchange rates they offered were at least 20 per cent better than advertised by the hostel. I selected a taxi driver – a red-turbaned Sikh – and he drove me somewhere discreet to make the transaction. As he handed his money over, he warned me that if the police turned up I should be prepared to run in both directions at once.

By now, we were ready to partake of some genuine Indian cooking. Our mouths were watering at the thought of all those delicious curries, tandooris, birianis and assorted relishes for which India is so famous. What we ended up getting, in the YMCA's gloomy restaurant, was a chicken curry – with no chicken in it. When we complained to the waiter, he fished around in the thin sauce and came up with a single sliver of chicken – about the size of a matchstick – which had been hiding behind a tomato. He gave us a triumphant grin.

Soon after coming into the vast circus of Connaught Place this evening, we attracted the attentions of a small, persistent beggar-girl. Her hair was lank and greasy, her nose was running with snot, and her whole body was painfully thin. She followed us halfway round the square, begging for just one rupee. Or the cost of a cup of coffee. What were we to do? Confronted by a tiny infant, her eyes wide with hunger, her clothes a single torn rag, her grimy little hand stretched out in a desperate plea for money, were we going to give her the price of her only meal of the day? Or were we going to be deterred by the many, many similarly impoverished and starving Indians all around, and simply turn her away?

No sooner had we 'paid off' the beggar girl, than we spotted three Indian workers wheeling a massive movie billboard up the road on a creaky old car. 'SEX AND THE ANIMALS!' shouted the poster slogan, 'THE MOST SIGNIFICANT PICTURE EVER MADE!' Astonished, we followed it down the road to see what was so significant about it. 'BANISHES MAN'S GUILT AND FEAR ABOUT SEX!' we read further, 'ANIMALS HAVE NO SHAME!' Proving the point, the rest of the billboard was full of tigers, horses and rhinoceroses all coupling away with big grins on their faces. We later learnt that this curious epic was the most popular film playing in India at the time – it was packing them out in every cinema throughout the country.

Stepping back in our amusement, we nearly fell down an open sewer. These gaping holes in the pavement, often full of fetid green excrement, are quite common in the area of Connaught Place. And it is very easy to fall down them, especially in the dark. Parts of this large circus are unbelievably filthy. One particular wall, for instance, ran about a hundred yards round the outermost circle of Connaught Place and had been turned into some sort of public toilet. Long lines of Indians were squatting down by it, as we passed, to relieve themselves.

We walked back to the lodge, through laughing throngs of nut-roasters, bicycle repair men and rickshaw drivers, noticing the beggars beginning to gather together round heaps of old smouldering tyres for warmth. Elsewhere, the many small herds of itinerant cows and bullocks were huddling up together also, mainly on the lawns of the public parks. It was a cold night.

January 4th

During a coach tour of the city this morning, our young Hindu guide suddenly became very excited. 'Look, there!' he pulled at my sleeve and pointed. All I could see was a hugely fat Sikh puttering past on a tiny motorbike. 'You are seeing?' exclaimed the guide. 'Is not this man looking *healthy?*'

The afternoon tour took us on to Old Delhi, stopping first at Laxmi Narayan Temple. The moment the bus stopped, we were surrounded by beggars, salesmen and traders. They all had just two things to sell – a road-map of India, and a pack of 'dirty postcards' which were actually just photos of erotic temple-carvings. To get rid of them, I bought the road-map and Kevin the dirty postcards. This freed us to watch a local snake-charmer trying to coax two sleepy cobras out of a basket. He didn't have a lot of luck. The snakes didn't like the cold, and slumped back into the basket moments after showing their faces.

At the back of the Red Fort, our final stop, I came across two young Hindus performing a levitation act. Lying under a large red sheet spread across the ground, they took it in turns to rise up in the air to a height of about twelve feet without any evidence of props. This spot, below the Fort and overlooking the Yamuna River, was apparently famous for local acts – rope-climbers, magicians, conjurers and dancing bears – being performed for the benefit of tourists. The Fort itself was also full of large monkeys. By the entrance of the Lahore Gate, I saw one of these inquisitive creatures assault a fat lady tourist and rob her of a bunch of bananas. Chased up the fortress walls by a fierce turbaned guard, it grinned back down on us from the battlements, a half-banana still jutting from its mouth like a Churchill cigar.

January 5th

This afternoon, we took a rickshaw into the old city of Delhi. We walked the final stretch along a long main road which had been turned into a street bazaar. The pavements were crowded with traders and salesmen selling clothes, books, watches, old boots, umbrellas, even complete sets of dentures. The iron railings by the footway were the province of astrologers, palmists, gurus, holy men, and sex specialists. This bazaar, we had earlier learnt, was also a favourite stamping ground for 'marriage brokers' who regarded foreign tourist as highly eligible prizes for their high-born clientele. Many Indian ladies, it seemed, would like nothing better than to marry a rich Englishman or American who would gain them a quick passage out of India. And it would be little use telling the broker you weren't rich. The very fact that you could afford to visit his country would be conclusive proof of your great wealth.

We cut across a park towards the Jami Masjid, the world's largest mosque, and were hailed by a succession of half-naked Indian masseurs sitting on rush mats, who were keen to give us a good massage and then to clean out our ears. Another tourist, whom we met later, told us that their services were actually very good.

What was not very good about the old city was its incredible squalor. Coming out of the central bazaar area of Chandni Chowk, we found ourselves in an impossible madhouse of congestion and noise. Adults and children alike were urinating and defecating on the streets, the public urinals having overflowed through overuse. Pitifully disfigured cripples huddled in doorways or in gutters. Scabrous rabid dogs – painfully thin and crawling with fleas – foraged weakly among the heaps of refuse. Cows and goats lay in their own dirt, swarming with flies and maggots. And into all this ploughed an urgent convoy of traffic, cutting a horn-powered swathe of din through the sea of human and animal debris and filth.

The bazaar itself was a full-scale assault on all the senses. The noise was deafening. The stench of rotting fish, vegetables and meat, and the acrid reek of offal, urine and sweat, was overpowering. And what we could see both fascinated and re-pelled us. In between heaped piles of excrement, legless crip-ples wheeled themselves about on fruit-box trolleys. On the mud-caked pavements, small swollen-stomached infants were dying of hunger. And everywhere we looked, hundreds of starving eyes followed us, begging money to relieve their mis-ery.

In the middle of a muddy swamp (which used to be a street) appeared the Hotel Relax. 'Welcome!' said its filth-splattered sign, 'Come Make Nice Comfortable Stay With Us!' The grin-ning old bandit at the door spat a jet of red *paan* (betel-nut juice) across the street and beckoned us eagerly inside, his gaze travelling covetously over our possessions. We nodded polite refusal, and continued on our way.

We next came across a flamboyant character mixing up what looked like raspberry-coloured puke in a huge cauldron. He was surrounded by a crowd of attentive Indians, all watch-ing his activity with silent, respectful interest. It turned out to be a cake-making demonstration. We stood and looked on for a while, and then a smartly-dressed young Hindu turned up and said, 'Hello. You are wanting hashish?' He made this surpris-ing offer in a loud tone, audible to half the crowd, and in the casual, offhand manner of someone offering a friend a ciga-rette. Kevin quickly drew me away from the scene. He had heard that many dope-dealers in the old city were in fact police informers.

Both of us returned to the hostel in a state of shock. Kevin, however, soon rallied to show me his surprise import into the country – a parcel containing ninety-two condoms. He then disappeared into town with two Italian schoolgirls, both of whom were devout Catholics and due out on the morning bus back to Rome. Kevin, I was coming to realise, was one of life's born optimists.

January 6th

This evening, we went to the Parsi Anjuman Hall, near Delhi Gate, to see an entertainment called 'Dances of India'. We were expecting great things of this, the programme having promised us 'Seventy-Five Minutes of Glorious Music, Dance and Song in all their Exquisite Finesse.'

When we came into the hall, we were surprised to see only seventeen other people in the audience. They were all shivering and huddled together for warmth, for the hall was very large and there was a gusty draught blowing through it. But then the show started, and everybody quickly forgot their discomfort. The skill and artistry of the dancers, performing many traditional Indian routines, soon held us spellbound with admiration. Particularly good, from our point of view, were the Peacock Dance (advertised as 'a Peacock in ECSTACY during the MONSOONS') and the Bhavai ('the Dancers PERFORM on Sharp Swords, Tumblers and Brass Plates with Seven POTS'). During the Bhavai, one of the dancers slipped on one of her brass plates and sent it spinning off into the wings like a flying saucer. To her great credit, she kept her balance perfectly. The Seven POTS on her head barely trembled.

The auto-rickshaw we took home was little more than a

motorcycle with a flimsy passenger canopy bolted over it. The suspension within was non-existent. Kevin and I bounced around inside the carriage like a couple of ricocheting bullets, and arrived back at the hostel with the fillings shaken loose from our teeth. The driver, by contrast, had spent the whole journey calmly leaning out of his cab, curious to see if his front wheel had fallen off yet.

January 7th

I spent this morning in the warm company of Mr Hardyal Sharma, a member of Nichiren Shoshu of India. This small, growing organisation marks the return of true Buddhism to the country of its origin after an absence of several hundred years, since being overshadowed by the Brahman pantheon of Hinduism. Founded by Shakyamuni (Gotama) Buddha some 3000 years ago, and revitalised by Nichiren Daishonin in 13th century Japan, Buddhism in its original, pure form is now again setting down firm roots in India.

I emerged from Mr Sharma's house in a dense fog, and it took me well over an hour to return to the YMCA. My rickshaw driver, despite his protests to the contrary, had no idea of where he was going. Having failed to persuade me out of the cab at the Nehru Planetarium, on the other side of town, he promptly reversed a mile back up the foggy highway (with no lights on) in an attempt to terrorise me out. He had evidently become tired of patrolling the city in the freezing mist and wanted to go home. Finally, he admitted he was quite lost and began taking directions from pedestrians. The last (of many) he asked told him that he had accidentally parked right outside the YMCA. He gave me a look of triumph, then enquired whether I had any dollars to sell.

Kevin I found in the restaurant, consoling an elderly woman tourist who had just had her bag and all her money stolen. She had only taken her eyes off the bag for a moment. Her story convinced Kevin that he would have to tighten up on his personal security. He presently wore a bulky body-belt – containing his money, travellers' cheques, airline ticket and passport – round his waist. But the woman had told him that this wasn't sufficient. Indian pickpockets were used to unzipping waist-belts and removing their contents without the wearer's knowledge. So Kevin decided he must locate the belt somewhere else on his person.

Back in our room, he stripped off and set to work. The belt began to work its way round his body like some kind of virulent spore. First it appeared round his right thigh, but this was no good. When he tried to walk, it simply slipped down around his ankles. Next, it turned up secured round his crotch. But this left him waddling round the room like a bandy-legged Gandhi. Then it settled round the base of his spine, just below his trouser-belt, but this felt like a truss. So he shifted it up to his chest. Now it looked like a pacemaker, and was strapped so tight he couldn't breathe. Finally, it came to rest under his left armpit, which was where I wore mine. But the belt was so bulky, that even with a shirt on, he looked grotesquely deformed.

Kevin confessed himself beaten, and returned the money-belt to his waist. To make it safe, however, he tied it to his person with so many pins, clips and padlocks as to foil even the most professional of thieves. The only problem was that Kevin couldn't access it himself. Later, when he wanted to buy a simple bar of chocolate, he had to enlist the shopkeeper, his assistant and myself to help him break into his own money!

January 8th

Today we set off on our three-day coach tour of Rajasthan, arguably India's most beautiful state. Breakfast was taken at a sleepy roadside restaurant along the way where bored elephants, moth-eaten camels and drowsy snakes were prodded into action for our benefit, then allowed to go back to sleep again.

Coming first to the Tomb of Akbar at Sikandra, we acquired a curious Indian guide with fond memories of the British Raj. He had a very military bearing, wore a swagger-stick under his arm, and sprinkled every sentence he uttered with quotations from Wordsworth or Shakespeare. His best contribution referred to the hordes of large wise-looking baboons scampering all around us. 'Attention!' he barked authoritatively. 'Many a slip betwixt cup and lip! If bit or scratched by monkey, go running immediate to doctor! Get anti-*rabbi* jab!'

Arriving next at Agra, the warm sun having now dispersed the chill from the air, we were again surrounded by an insistent troop of salesmen, this time selling cheap plaster models of the Taj Mahal. Nobody was interested. We all wanted to see the real thing. And we were not disappointed. Our first glimpse of this incredible 'monument to love' dispelled all our doubts regarding its reputation. The massive white marble structure glittered like a priceless jewel in the bright midday sun, and was equally perfect to my eye whether viewed from afar or right up close. As for the interior, a note of pathos was sounded by the twin tombs of Emperor Shahjahan and his wife Mumtaz. It is said that Shahjahan, prevented from draining the public coffers further by building a tomb of his own (a replica of the Taj, in black marble) and locked up for many years by his son should he attempt it, finally elected to be buried alongside his beloved wife instead.

Proceeding on, I put my camera out of the bus window for a quick snap of the street bazaars. To my surprise, the whole street ground to a halt. Every Indian in sight stopped whatever he or she was doing, and posed for the camera. Then, the shot taken, they instantly resumed their busy, noisy activity. Later, coming out of the magnificent 'ghost city' of Fatehpur Sikri (deserted by its vast population after just 17 years, when the water-wells ran dry), another odd incident occurred. A young boy came up to offer me a charming marble statue in return for my socks. I padded back to the bus in my bare feet.

At our lodgings that evening, the Bharatpur Tourist Bunga-low, we all crowded round the restaurant's single one-bar heater and anxiously waited for some hot food to warm us up. The night was becoming increasingly cold. A breakfast menu appeared on our table, and I studied it. We were given a choice of PORDGE and CORN-FLEX, followed by BED TEA. Then there was SAND WITCHES, to be followed by MANGO FOUL and CARAMEL CUSTERED.

Finally, the waiter appeared and asked us what we would like. We returned the menu and told him, but he didn't have any of it. He just waggled his head sorrowfully and said to everybody, 'So sorry, this is not possible.' He couldn't tell us why it was not possible, just that it wasn't. We couldn't under-stand it. Then Kevin said, 'Look, forget about what we want. What have you *got?*' That did the trick. The waiter nodded furiously and replied, 'Meals!'

In India, 'meals' are often another name for *thalis*. Our *thalis* arrived on large metal platters, and comprised a large heap of plain rice (cold) in the centre, surrounded by five small dishes of curried vegetables, chillies and curd. Most of us, un-used to such food, gave the 'meals' a miss and sucked listlessly on our chapatis instead. Only one of our number, a ruddy-faced Australian, finished his food completely. He couldn't speak highly enough of *thalis*. He assured us that we would all get used to them in time. Kevin looked at him as if he was crazy.

January 9th

Dawn saw us trudging down to the Bharatpur Bird Sanctuary in the freezing fog. Our guide told us that this was the best time of day to view the rare and exotic birds, but none of us could see anything. There was only one bird enthusiast in our party, a myopic Indian who stalked the guide relentlessly in his hope of seeing some rare snipe or giant crane. This hope dashed by the thick mist over the marshy lake-land, he settled for going duck-spotting. 'Ah, over there!' he would declare at regular intervals. 'Dat is a *mallarrrrd*!' And the guide would nod at him indulgently, even when (and this was often) it wasn't a mallard at all.

'Excuse me,' asked Kevin over breakfast, 'but where does your milk come from?' The waiter stared at the thick brown scum of oily globules floating on Kevin's coffee, and replied: 'Baboon.'

Relaxing this afternoon on the lush green lawns of Sariska Tourist Bungalow, I watched all the others leave on a bus to the nearby nature reserve. They all wanted to see Sariska's famous White Tiger. Hours later, they returned tired and disillusioned. They hadn't seen anything at all, let alone the White Tiger. The bus had roared through the reserve at such speed that every animal they passed had instantly scurried for cover. All that Kevin had seen was a couple of wild pigs (who tried to head butt the bus), a rhinoceros (asleep) and a peacock (dead). The bus had finally screeched to a halt at a Monkey Temple, where the guide told everybody to go in, dong a big bell, and pray to the Monkey God for the White Tiger to appear. But nothing happened. Later on, we discovered that the last White Tiger seen in these parts had been captured years ago, and was now a stuffed exhibit in a Delhi museum.

Over supper, I met a statuesque Australian girl called Anna, who had just wasted the last two months waiting in Tibet for the Dalai Lama to show up. She said he was as difficult to see as the White Tiger. Then she introduced her 'companion', a small Indian man to whom she was trying to teach English. On parting, he kindly offered to show me a 'good time' when we next met. Corrected on his poor phrasing by Anna, he apologised and said, 'So sorry! I mean I *enjoy* you next time!'

I was joined in the cold, empty drinks lounge later by the reception clerk. He was a swarthy, grinning man with bad teeth. After telling me all about his crippled grandmother, his suffering wife and his hungry children, he offered me a hashish cigarette. Then he snuggled up close, and offered me a share of his blanket. Nervous, I went off to my room. He tried to follow me in, but the sound of Kevin's loud snores within managed to deter him. I came to my bed tired, but was unable to sleep. Outside my window, what sounded like a hundred cats were yowling away in unearthly chorus. In the morning, I found out they hadn't been cats at all, but peacocks.

January 10th

Our bus driver excelled himself this morning. In the course of his usual game of 'dare' with speeding buses coming the other

15

way, he managed to nudge a camel and cart down a deep ditch. All the Indian tourists aboard thought this highly amusing, and shouted up hearty congratulations.

The first stop today was the Amber Palace, near Jaipur. Set atop a high hill, this magnificent structure glowed like a bright yellow pearl against an impressive backdrop of rugged hillside watchtowers and fortifications. Walking up, we came through a small garden seething with giant rats. A couple of New Zealanders with us explained that the rat (and the peacock) were worshipped as animal divinities in Rajasthan. They recalled a visit to the famous Rat Temple in Bikaner, where the priests hadn't let them in until they had taken off their shoes. Consequently, when they had entered the temple courtyard, scores of wild rats began scuttling over their bare feet and running up their trouserlegs.

On the way home to Delhi, we stopped at a 'halfway house' tea-shop which had been set up by the Rajasthan Tourist Board to encourage tourism. I patiently waited through the tea queue, but was sent away to buy a 'tea coupon'. So I patiently waited through the tea coupon queue, but then found the coupon man had gone for his own tea. I patiently waited for him to return, and then he gave me a marmalade toast coupon by mistake. So I had to come back and start queuing all over again. Then the coupon man couldn't give me a tea coupon, because all I had was a torn two-rupee note which he couldn't change. Kevin finally lent me the money, and I got the tea coupon. The glorious words 'One tea!' floated back to the kitchen, and I thought I was in business. But then there was a power-cut, and when the lights came back on the tea-man had lost my coupon and I had to queue up for another one. By this time, the bus was impatiently hooting for our return and I had to forget the whole thing.

January 11th

Visiting the Odeon cinema in Connaught Place, we caught the 10am matinee showing of *The Blue Lagoon* in English. The audience turned out to be just as interesting as the film. Mostly Indian men in their 20s and 30s, they took a strangely lascivious delight in this innocent story of two children growing up and falling in love on a desert island. We knew that in their own films, hero and heroine were not allowed to even kiss onscreen, but the attention these two scantily-clad children received whenever they embraced or revealed bare flesh was amazing. The audience were quite beside themselves with suppressed excitement, and giggled and pointed throughout the picture. Then, just five minutes from the end - with the children being rescued and set to recover some clothing – everyone rose in unison and made a noisy exit from the cinema. When the lights came on, Kevin and I found ourselves in an empty auditorium. Well, not quite empty – there was an usher present. But he was lying fast asleep over the rear seats.

This evening, Kevin tried phoning a girl he had met on the Rajasthan tour. But he couldn't get through. He spent two long hours at the phone, and ended up having a strange conversation with a cake-shop owner in Connaught Place.

Some people do manage to use India's internal phone system successfully though. We'd heard someone having a *very* successful phone call at 5 o'clock this morning. It was an Indian guest using the public phone on our floor. He was shouting down the receiver so loudly that everybody on our corridor woke up. Each time he came to the end of a sentence, he uttered a booming '*HA, HA, HA!*' Which made us wonder why he needed a phone at all.

January 12th

We moved out of the YMCA at noon today, and went in search of a Hindi film to pass the time while we waited for tonight's train down to Madras. Most cinemas we came to had the 'House Full' sign up, and were fully booked three days ahead. We began to realise the enormous popularity movies had in India. Then we came to one cinema, the Plaza, where tickets still remained. We joined a long queue of Indian men, none of whom knew what they were queuing up for. We questioned many of them, but nobody we asked knew the title of the film, what it was about, or even what time it started.

This was the first Hindi picture either of us had ever seen, and it was really rather good. It depicted the lives of three Indian women from varying castes and social backgrounds, and described the ways in which they inter-related. The first of the women was very rich, very bored and slept a lot. The second went out to work, was married to an alcoholic husband, and suffered constant abuse from a mother-in-law. The third was a lowly servant, afflicted by the continual bad moods and childish petulance of the other two. It was all very interesting, but we couldn't help thinking what a difficult place India must be for women, no matter what their background.

We reached New Delhi station at 6.30pm, and boarded the Grand Trunk Express bound for Madras. In view of the very lengthy (thirty-six hours) nature of this journey, we had decided to travel First Class, in air-conditioned sleeper berths. This was a mistake. We should have taken the Chair Car accommodation, but it was too late to think of that. We found ourselves in a carriage full of boisterous Indian athletes, all singing rock and roll songs. If this was not enough, we found our berths to be a simple six-by-three bare plank apiece. The prospect of lying on this for the next day and a half was daunting. To console himself, Kevin ordered some train food. It turned out to be yet another *thali*, and he disconsolately threw it out of the window. Our Indian friends ceased singing at 10.30pm, and the lights went out. Then, just as I was asleep, one of them began having a loud nightmare and I woke up again. It was to be a long, long night.

January 13th

The morning began with all the Indian athletes bellowing morning greetings across to each other from their bunks. Caught in the crossfire, we woke up. Kevin went for a stroll, and returned to tell me that we had been stuck in Vidisha station the past two hours, owing to a train being derailed further up the line. And a further three-hour delay was expected.

Leaning out of our window, we spotted a wizened old chawallah beetling up and down the platform, carrying a large aluminium teapot and a box full of earthenware teacups. As we waved and tried to gain his attention, a hail of these disposable teacups – their contents finished – began to rain down on the platform. The little old man dodged this continual flak of missiles, and picked his way through the broken crockery to serve us our teas with an air of resigned stoicism.

News of our further delay had now swept through the train. Every Indian aboard promptly swarmed onto the platform to clean their teeth. There were about six enamel double-sinks along the platform, and each one was soon surrounded by a jostling crowd of Indians brandishing their toothbrushes.

Eventually, the train moved off. Then it stopped again. Then it started, and stopped and started. By noon, we were running five hours late. Passing through Bhopal, the weather was becoming noticeably warmer, and as we pushed on southward the heat continued to gain in strength. Between Itarsi and Betel, the guard shut all the doors to the train. He informed us that this stretch was notorious for bandit-attacks on passing trains.

It was otherwise an uneventful journey. We ate a freshly cooked omelette on Nagpur platform, and very little else. Most of the time, we just played cards with the Indian athletes, or lay for hours on end on our tiny bunks, imagining the walls closing in on us. We wondered if this journey would ever end.

January 14th

I've changed my mind. The nearest thing to purgatory for the tourist in this country is not waiting in an endless train reservation queue. It is lying endlessly in a tiny coffin-bunk in a so-called express train now running six hours late. I woke up feeling I had been on this train all my life. My whole world had shrunk to a cramped compartment six feet square. Apart from the occasional cigarette break on a station platform, the outside world might as well never have existed.

Our Indian fellow-passengers livened things up for a while by teaching us how to eat *thalis*. They had caught Kevin trying to throw another *thali* out of the window, and forced him to try eating it the 'Indian' way. This involved Kevin mixing all the rice, curried vegetables, chillies and peppers together in a big steaming heap of yellow mush, and then stuffing it down his throat in large dripping handfuls, muttering the while that he couldn't remember ever having eaten anything so tasty.

We arrived in Madras forty-one claustrophobic hours after

leaving Delhi. It was noon, and the heat was intense. We stumbled off the train feeling like two convicts unexpectedly reprieved from Alcatraz. Kevin's face, I observed, was deathly pale. He looked like Lazarus recently recalled from the grave.

Madras station was a nightmare of noise, heat and unpleasant smells. We struggled quickly out, and went in search of quiet, clean lodgings. All we managed to find – it being a festival day and most places being full or closed – was the AVC Hotel in JB Street. This place was cheap but was obviously not used to Western tourists. Our room-boy, a burn-black Indian wearing a *lunghi* (sarong) and a permanent grin, was so fascinated with us that he followed us into our quarters and stayed there. Kevin temporarily shifted him by ordering a cup of black coffee, without sugar. The room-boy presently returned with a cup of white tea, with sugar. He beamed happily at Kevin, and Kevin glared banefully back. It was the beginning of a beautiful friendship.

The room-boy was particularly fascinated by my dirty laundry, which had just been unpacked. He couldn't keep his eyes off it. I concluded that he must be the *dhobi-wallah* eager to wash it, so I stuffed the lot in his arms and said 'Please do *dhobi.*' His response was quite extraordinary. Giving a groan of emotion, he sank to his knees to kiss my feet, then retreated out of the room muttering 'Presentation! Presentation!' to himself. Kevin informed me that I just made a present of all my clothes to the room-boy. He was prepared to bet I would never see them again.

I saw the room-boy again though, and only minutes later. After Kevin had retired to his room, I shut my door and collapsed on my bed, pleased to be quite alone for once. But then I looked up at the ceiling, and found that I wasn't alone at all. There was a yellow lizard staring down at me. We gazed at each other for a while, and then I got bored of waiting for it to drop on my head, and called back the room-boy to get rid of it. He came in waving a broom and proceeded to chase the lizard all over the room. Then he opened the door to let it out, and instead let another one in. I now had two yellow lizards.

Later, Kevin and I went out for some lunch, and found a good Chinese restaurant set back from Mount Road. On the entrance door, a curious sign announced:

'We have been in this Business since long, and we have been pleasing and displeasing our customers ever since. We have been bawled out, bailed up, held up and held down, cussed and discussed, recommended and boycotted, talked to and about, burned up and burned out etc. The only reason we continue to stay in business is to see what in hell could possibly happen next!'

Eating our meal on the pleasant upper-storey, open-air verandah, we noticed many large black rooks flying in and out to dine on leftovers off the dining tables. Kevin observed them hopping his way, and polished off every scrap of food on his plate. He wasn't going to leave them anything.

Back at the lodge, the companionable room-boy turned up again, this time to beg my best shirt off my back. I only got rid of him by taking him by the shoulders and steering him bodily out of my room. He sat outside the door and went to sleep. Except for the lizards, I was now alone. But I was feeling very hot, and decided to turn on the overhead air-fan. This was a serious error. It had only one speed – very fast indeed. Within seconds, it was whizzing round like an aeroplane propeller. A hurricane blast of air blew me off my feet and pinned me to the bed. The yellow lizard on the ceiling was plucked off its perch and sent flying across the room. Struggling up and turning the fan off again, I found the lizard lying stunned on the floor of the squat toilet. It remained in a state of concussion for the rest of the afternoon.

This evening's stroll produced a visit to a local Hindu temple, hidden down the end of a dark, narrow backstreet. An elderly priest wearing the marks of Vishnu (vertical lines of red and white paint) on his forehead showed us around. As he proudly opened up all the shrines for viewing, he told us that today was a big festival day, and this was why all the god-figures wore garlands of flowers around their necks.

On the way out, the old man bowed to us and we bowed back. Then he felt compelled to bow again, and so we felt obliged to give another bow. This went on for some time, the three of us bobbing up and down on the temple steps, until the priest broke the monotony by suddenly darting off to get us a 'present'. This turned out to be a bowlful of very bitter berries which we had to eat in front of him with every appearance of delight. Downing several cups of tea later on, we decided not to take any more 'presents' from anybody for the time being.

January 15th

A toothless old man in a dirty dhoti turned up at 8am, armed with a broom and a bucket. He wanted to clean out the squat toilet. First he removed the concussed lizard and then, when my back was turned, he removed a pack of my disposable razors.

Another old man, this time a rickshaw driver cycling us up to Madras station, proved so feeble that we had to get out at every hill and give him a push up. By the time we creaked into the station, he looked so ruined that Kevin was all for calling out an ambulance.

The whole population of Madras seemed to be out on the streets today, celebrating the Spring Harvest Festival called 'Pongol'. Many people we saw were either waving bunches of bananas about in the air, or carefully painting the horns of sacred cows. They were painting them every colour of the rainbow – one poor beast we saw had one horn daubed bright purple, and the other green and red with blue polka-dots. As we watched, a crowd of noisy children stuck a large lemon and a bunch of lighted faggots on the painted horns, and began chasing the smouldering cow down the road shouting what sounded to us like "bugger! bugger!" after it as they gave gleeful pursuit.

Later, we walked down to the coastline and went swimming off Elliot's Beach. The sea here was warm, clear and refreshing, and the huge waves sweeping into land shocked us instantly out of our heat lethargy, and left our skin all a tingle. Back on the beach and drying off, we were surrounded by a crowd of curious locals. They appeared to be waiting for something. Moments later, the tide suddenly came in and we were deluged by a large wave. The waiting crowd erupted into loud laughter.

Wandering damply back to town, we came across another decorated cow. This one wore garlands of yellow flowers on its horns and had little brass bells tied round its forelegs. It was contentedly eating a pile of refuse in the gutter. We stepped round it and a local cha-shop. It was occupied by a boisterous gang of Muslim youths who insisted on buying us endless cups of very sweet tea. Kevin tried to protest that he didn't like sugar, but they didn't believe him. Everybody in India liked sugar, they said, and lots of it.

Our new friends wanted to hear everything we knew about English cricket and British motorbikes. But neither of us knew anything about either subject, so it was a very short conversation. Undeterred, the inquisitive party moved on to the subject of marriage. They couldn't believe we were still unmarried. There was so much *opportunity* to get married in the West. Surely, they insisted, we could *afford* it?

Madras, we concluded by the end of today's tour, is a strange city. The Indians here stop and stare at you all the time, and often follow you down the street. Tiny children pass by riding adult bicycles bigger than they are. Entire families of four or five people putter along on single 50cc mopeds. Herds of goats tied together with string wander aimlessly round in the middle of the traffic. Holy cows are allowed to graze and defecate on the lawns of plush banks and hotels. And groups of destitute women and children sleep in carts, on car bonnets, or simply in the gutters. The contrast between affluence and poverty, with lines of beggars sitting outside the best hotels, is in this city extremely marked.

January 16th

We decided to look for better lodgings today. But this was easier said than done. The room-boy, as expected, refused to return my laundry. So I had to refuse to pay the bill. The laundry promptly reappeared, minus a pair of red underpants. The room-boy had taken a particular shine to these. Nothing I said could persuade him to part with them.

After a long search, we found good rooms at the YMCA hostel in Pycrofts Road. My quarters here were clean and comfortable, and there wasn't a lizard in sight. I did have problems with the air-fan again, though. This one didn't work at all.

I went down to the rickshaw-rank to get a ride further down

Pycrofts Road to the house of another Buddhist contact, Venkat Sai. None of the six rickshaw drivers I asked knew where Pycrofts Road was, even though they were sitting in it. Then a doddering old greybeard creaked up and faithfully *promised* he knew the way. He promptly swung off Pycrofts Road and got himself thoroughly lost. Then he took a lot of directions from passers-by, and got himself thoroughly confused. But all this didn't deter him, just made him more resolute. He peddled off into the great unknown with such sense of clear purpose that I didn't dare accuse him of not knowing where he was going. An hour later however, and having arrived right back where we'd started, I changed my mind. I got out of the rickshaw, thanked him for his guided tour of the city, and walked to my destination.

In the afternoon, Kevin and I decided to change some money at the Indian Overseas Bank. We sat at a desk marked 'travellers cheques' and waited for ten minutes. Then someone came over to tell us that this desk didn't deal with travellers' cheques at all. He showed us to another desk. This one *didn't* have a sign saying 'travellers cheques', so we guessed we must be in business. We handed our passports to the desk-clerk, and he stared down at them. That's all he did, just stared at them. Five tense minutes ticked past. Then he stopped staring at them, and gave them to another official to stare at. Both men wore such looks of intense concentration that we wondered if they'd ever seen a British passport before. The second official, suddenly aware of Kevin's teeth grinding with frustration, emerged from his trance and returned the passports to the first official, who gave a short grunt and pushed a large heap of forms over to us to fill out. All we got for wading through this lot was a small brass token each. Kevin's bore the number 22, and mine 29. The indicator panel above the paydesk, we noted with dismay, had just clicked to the number 49. By the time it had worked its way up to 100, and then gone from zero to our numbers, the rest of the day would be gone.

But then the indicator clicked again. It moved straight from 49 to Kevin's number. Relieved, we collected our money, and asked for a receipt. But the paydesk didn't issue receipts. It told us to go back to our friends with the fixation on passports, to get one. And surprise, surprise, both officials had just gone for lunch.

January 18th

Something will have to be done about these mosquitoes. Sleep was quite impossible last night. Persistent squadrons of these little bloodsuckers were diving down on me till 4 in the morning. In the end, I shut all doors and windows (ignoring the stifling heat) and lit up three 'Tortoise' mosquito-repellent coils. The packet promised they would drive the little monsters into a 'deep swoon'. An hour later, with room enveloped in a dense blanket of smoke, it didn't matter whether the mosquitoes swooned or not. They couldn't even find me! Comforted by this thought, I finally swooned myself.

Lack of sleep made this a difficult day. Apart from which, this was a Friday and all Madras's sightseeing spots were closed. The only place open, we were informed, was Fort St George. But when we arrived there, this was closed too. We sat on an anthill and drank an insipid cup of coffee. Then we found one place not closed – the charming 18th century St Mary's Church. This attractive structure had stone flooring tiled with gravestones, marvellous pillar-work and mosaic–patterned ceilings. The only thing that disturbed us was all the signs prophesying a nuclear war.

The enervating heat diminished Kevin's conversation to a minimum today. He restricted himself to two phrases only: 'Why isn't your meter working?' (addressed to taxi-drivers), and 'Has that water been boiled?' (addressed to waiters fond of drawing table-water from next to open sewers). Otherwise, he was quite silent. Kevin had become tired of remonstrating with legions of beggars. Now he simply walked through them. Or, if necessary, over them. They seemed to respect that.

This evening we saw a quack doctor selling health cures on the street. First he used a loud football klaxon to attract a crowd, then he seized a 'volunteer' from the audience and held him captive with a pair of prison manacles while he poured a bottle of health tonic down his throat.

Moving on, we came across another crowd, this time piled into the entrance of a television shop. Everybody was pressed against the window watching a television set – something few of them would ever possess – being demonstrated to a customer. On the screen, a fat middle-aged Indian in incredibly tight trousers was rolling up a ski-slope backwards, singing a number one pop ballad. The massed crowds standing outside wore a uniform look of awed appreciation. They had never seen anything like it. Neither had we.

January 19th

We left the heat and chaos of Madras this morning, and travelled down to the peaceful coastal haven of Mahabilapuram. A rickshaw driver turned up at the bus depot, and offered us lodgings in his own house. We ended up with a small bare stone cell in an adjoining thatched hut. The cost was remarkably low – just three rupees (20 pence) each per night. Our 'neighbours' were a young couple called John and Suki, who had lived in India some years and who had gone quite ethnic in their dress. John, a dreamy loquacious individual, wore a small fez glistening with semi-precious stones, long flowing robes and a number of exotic beads and necklace. Suki was decked out in a bright ruby-red sari and had applied a thick layer of *kohl* to her eyes and cheekbones. As we arrived, she was playing a local folk song to her baby daughter, Kali, on an antique squeezebox.

John's milky blue eyes glistened with emotion as he learnt that Kevin was from Suffolk, only a few miles from his own home town in England. He squatted outside our hut like a mischievous pixie and plied Kevin with an endless stream of questions about life back home. Meanwhile, I had finally located the switch to our single light-bulb, and had noticed that our cell had no furniture in it. Not even a bed. But that was okay, said John, for everyone here slept on the porch outside. It was so much cooler.

Kevin and I went up a winding dirt-track leading up to the beach. Across our path scurried a number of small, grunting pigs, while tiny green frogs leapt in and out of discarded coconut shells. Thirsty dogs lay in doorways, tongues lolling out with the heat. Naked children ran past, rolling old bicycle tyres and cheerfully laughing. Householders sat on their porches, giving us a lazy wave of welcome. The sun shone brightly, and a warm sea-breeze caressed our necks and shoulders. Yes, Mahabilapuram was going to suit us fine.

Up this road, we discovered the Village Restaurant. Not only did it have a good selection of Western music, but both its waiters could speak good English. One of them produced a giant lobster on a plate, and offered it to Kevin. The lobster snapped hopefully at Kevin's nose, but he didn't want it. So the waiter stuck it by the entrance, hoping that some hungry passer-by might spot it. The lobster sat obediently on its plate and waved its powerful purple claws about in enthusiastic welcome to prospective customers. But nobody accepted the invitation, and it presently sank into a dejected sulk. To wake it up again, the waiter came over and began plucking its eyeballs. The lobster promptly returned from the dead.

Coming out onto Mahabilapuram's glorious beach, we spotted its famous Shore Temple. The guide we hired told us that this was the last of seven original sea-temples built by the Dravidian architects of the 7th century AD. The other six had already been consumed by the hungry sea, and this one would soon experience the same fate. Its only protection was a buttress-wall of large boulders, already much weakened by the continuous battering of incoming breakers.

Undeterred by the news that the previous occupant of our hut (a young American girl) had drowned here last week, we plunged into the sea and found it excellent for swimming. Even Kevin, not generally fond of the water, enjoyed romping around in these waves. They helped him forget about the thirty-six mosquito bites on his left arm.

It was impossible to be alone for long on this beach, though. Kevin managed to lose a grinning fisherman trying to sell him a brace of snapping lobsters by claiming to be vegetarian, but he hit real problems with his next visitor. This was a gap-toothed, shifty-eyed pirate –wearing just a ragged bandana and a soiled lunghi – who sat behind us for a whole hour, banging two coconuts together. You can't imagine what the sound of two coconuts being banged together does to your nerves after a while. The grinning rogue selling them did, though. And when Kevin at last gave in, he uttered a shrill cackle of triumph and began beheading the green coconuts with a razor-sharp machete. The milk within was unpalatably sweet, but the two rupees apiece we had paid was a small price to get rid of the noise.

After an excellent supper at the Village Restaurant – which this evening was crowded with long-stay travellers and hippies dressed in colourful kaftans, baggy silk trousers and patterned waistcoats – we walked around the sleepy village's only two main streets. All the local Indians here were either chipping away on stone sculptures for tourist sale, or coming up to ask us: 'You have English coins for my collection?'

We returned to the seashore to view the sea-temple by night. Except for the regular wash of the waves, it was completely quiet. The temple glowed luminous-white in the reflected light of the rising moon. The sky was clear as a bell, and a fresh, clean breeze was blowing in from the sea. We sat on the temple steps, and began to feel the calm, tranquil atmosphere stealing over us and soothing our souls.

Suddenly, a strident voice broke the silence. 'Gidday!' it said. 'Where's the action?'

The voice belonged to a lively, lanky Australian called Gill, who had brought his English friend Jim out for a night stroll.

'I've brought this whingeing Pom for a glim of the temple!' explained Gill. 'He absolutely _hates_ temples. I've dragged him round every temple in South India!'

Then he began complaining about the lack of action again, and dragged us all off to a tea-stall in town where he reckoned 'it all happens' on a Saturday night.

Once at the tea-stall, Gill leapt forward to exclaim: 'Okay, where's the dancing girls?' The old crone manning the tea-urn gazed at him in mute incomprehension. As well she might, for there were no dancing girls, there was no 'action', there was nothing happening here at all. Apart, that is, for six huddled Indians drinking tea and a local cow trying to climb under a low tea table.

Gill entertained us with stories of his visit to Goa. Most of the outside toilets in Goa, he informed us, had pig farms built below them. On his first trip to one of these, Gill got a nasty shock. He'd just squatted down to lower his backside over the hole in the floor (the toilet), when a low, hungry snort below him made him look between his legs. He saw a pair of beady, piggy eyes eagerly waiting for him to supply breakfast.

'They just love foreign shit, those pigs do!' recalled Gill. 'They don't move an inch when an Indian goes for a crap, but when they see a tourist coming, they're up and off and forming a queue under that toilet with their napkins on before he's even crossed the street!'

Kevin and I slept tonight on the porch outside our hut, sharing a tiny mattress lent us by the landlord. It provided very little padding against the bare stone floor. And for a while at least, we were busily occupied fending off invasions of ants, beetles, cockroaches and hopping frogs – all coming from the banana plantation in the nearby garden. For once, however, there were no mosquitoes.

January 21st

We arrived at the Village Restaurant this morning before the staff had woken up. Whilst waiting for them to get dressed, we discovered the establishment's beautiful back garden and took turns lying in its hammock, watching the world go by.

The view from the hammock was marvellous – an inland lake, calm and serene; rustic cottages and reed huts dotting the far bank; rows of lush green palm trees and banks of reeds all around, rustling gently in the cool morning breeze.

The whole day followed suit, tranquil and quiet. Even the waves pounding into the shore seemed somehow less angry, less tempestuous. We lay on the beach and did nothing at all. I remarked to Kevin that we couldn't afford to stay in Mahabilapuram long. It was so pleasant, we might never leave.

January 22nd

The mosquitoes arrived last night. Having remembered to put on 'Odomos' repellent, I woke up refreshed. But Kevin and our new neighbour, Nick, didn't wake up refreshed at all. They had both been plagued by the little vampires all night. The rest of the day, their covetous, envious eyes followed me everywhere, mentally appropriating my small tube of protective cream.

Over breakfast, tears came to Kevin's eyes as he fought the temptation to scratch his numerous bites. He knew that if he started, he would end up flaying himself alive. So he sweated things out in moody, monastic silence until the irritation drove him out to the garden hammock, where he swung back and forth in restless bad spirits.

Sometimes I don't credit Kevin. I mean, it's one thing to stroll around unprotected like a walking lunch for mosquitoes. But it's quite another to lie around all day unprotected against the fierce sun, stubbornly refusing to use any cream or oil. He returned to the hut tonight looking like a large red blister. I had never seen such a bad case of sunburn. But I had to hand it to Kevin. He has such a remarkable facility for laughing at vicissitude. His entire body burned raw-red and pocked with livid mosquito scars, he told me he was now coming down with flu into the bargain. But did all this deflate him? None of it. 'You know something?' he remarked over supper. 'I don't believe I've ever felt better in my life!'

The conversation came back to the subject of Goa.

'One guy I knew,' recalled John, 'got the dysentery real bad in Goa. A doctor gave him an opium tablet to stick up his backside. But he'd no sooner done this than he got another attack and shot out to the squat-toilet. Well, of course there was this pig waiting down below, and it ate everything that came down – including the opium tablet. An hour of so later, the pig's owners found it lying on its back in the high street of Goa, kicking its little legs in the air and snorting fit to burst. 'Man,' declared my friend, 'that's about the happiest-looking pig I _ever_ saw!'

January 23rd

I woke suddenly in the dead of night, surrounded by smoke. I had set my mattress on fire. It had been ignited by the 'Tortoise' ring I had lit by my head to keep the mosquitoes away. It took two water-bottles to douse the fire completely, yet the damage was done. I was now left with two problems – how to explain to the landlord the charred lump missing out of his personal mattress, and where to sleep tonight, for the surviving section of it was now a waterlogged ruin. I decided to go for a walk.

It was 3am when I ambled up to the sea-temple. The moon was down, and it was pitch-black. For a while, it was easy to imagine myself the last person on Earth. But then, out of a dark recess of the temple ruins, came a voice. 'Master!...Rajah!' it hissed, '...you have *cigarette?*'

The mattress was only slightly damp by the time I returned, so I got some sleep after all. The landlord was not at all pleased when the burnt, sodden bedding came to his attention later on. He did an angry little jig on the forecourt, shouting, 'Look! Firing! Firing!' My apologies fell on deaf ears; he was quite inconsolable.

The Village Restaurant was absolutely packed tonight. Kevin had told everybody he'd met that this was the only place in town to get a decent cup of coffee. But the restaurant just wasn't geared to handle 29 customers at once. The staff simply couldn't cope. The young waiter, Charlie – normally so cool, calm and collected – was reduced to tears by the continual barrage of food orders. Imbal, a young Israeli girl we'd met earlier, sent me into the cookhouse to see what had happened to the lime lassi she'd ordered two hours previously. I found the cook spread senseless over the utensils cupboard; the pressure of work had driven him to drink. He had been trying to cook 29 suppers on two small electric hot-plates! On the way out, I found Imbal's lime lassi. Charlie had made it an hour and half ago, but had forgotten to bring it in.

Fed up with waiting, Kevin had been consulting the rest of the guests. He called Charlie over, and told him we had all changed our orders to make things simpler. All he had to do now, said Kevin, was dish up 29 fresh boiled lobsters. Charlie looked at him aghast, and closed the restaurant.

January 24th

We reluctantly left Mahabilapuram today, and took a bus on to Kanchipuram.

There, we found lodgings at the Raja Lodge, close to the bus-stand, and went in search of food. Having had enough of *thalis* by now, we were looking for the only place in town reputed to have something different – the New Madras Hotel.

Along the way, we took stock of Kanchipuram itself. It was without doubt the noisiest Indian centre we had visited. Its busy streets were full of giant public carriers, the constant blast of their air-horns jangling our nerves and setting our teeth on edge. The air-horns were even left on when the vehicles were parked. As for the many shops and stores along the streets, these were either constructed from planks of uneven timber or from uneven sheets of corrugated tin. The place gave the general impression of a struggling shanty-town – heaving both with people and sacred cows. I had never seen so many cows packed into one place.

It took us a long hour to track down the New Madras Hotel. It should have taken us just ten minutes. None of the locals spoke any English. They did their best – every few steps a grinning Indian turned up to offer us a rickshaw ride or to give us some wrong directions – but we kept ending up back at the Raja Lodge. It was uncanny. And when we did come to the New Madras Hotel, it was a sheer fluke.

The restaurant was something of a disappointment. It had a rather dirty, greasy, seedy atmosphere. But it certainly had some character too. I had just received my egg biriani and stuffed paratha (spelt 'stuffed parrot' on the menu), when Kevin discovered a rat under his chair. He promptly leapt up and started a jig of alarm on the table. A party of Indians at the adjacent table, guessing that he was treating them to an impromptu English dance display, began stamping their feet and cheering him on with claps and whistles. By this time, the rat had disappeared. So had Kevin's dinner. He had sent it flying when he'd jumped on the table.

January 25th

We were awoken in the morning by the Indian party occupying the rooms all around us shouting good morning to each other across the corridor. This racket commenced at 5am. These were the same Indians who had been shouting good night to each other until 12 the previous night. We wondered how they managed on just five hours sleep. We also wondered why they felt obliged to impose the same ascetic regime on poor, weary travellers like ourselves.

The morning's breakfast – a cup of coffee and a bun – was taken at a roadside cha-house. We sat on a low wooden bench, our feet covered in a black moving carpet of flies emerging from the nearby gutters. It was decided to make a move as soon as possible.

Hailing a cycle-rickshaw, we contracted a rate of Rs15 (35 pence) to see Kanchipuram's three most distinguished temples. After visiting the Kailasanathar (devoted to Shiva) and the imposing Kamakshiamon (dedicated to Shiva's wife, Parvati), we came at last to the Ekambareswarer temple, which was fronted by an outstanding tower 57 metres in height. This particular temple has quite a poor reputation amongst tourists – beggars, cripples, even priests gather from miles around to hassle visitors for money.

The cripples here were the most deformed and pitiful we had yet seen. Elephantiasis is a common affliction in these parts, being easily contracted by walking barefoot in the city's flyblown streets – the worms bore into the soles of the feet, and work their way up through the bloodstream to bloat the legs or the testicles to gigantic proportions. One victim of this appalling disease lay against a temple pillar, unable to walk. His right leg was swollen to the size of a tree-trunk. Another unfortunate passed close by, cupping testicles as big as melons between his hands. He was quite naked. It was only when I saw this that I recalled John's story, told us in Mahabilapuram, of seeing a man wheeling his genitals down the road in a wheelbarrow – and mentally admonished myself for not taking him seriously at the time.

Back on the streets in the afternoon, we were soon worn down by an everlasting stream of Indian men pestering us with questions. They wanted to know our names, whether we were married, why we weren't married, what our jobs were, and how much we earned. They were keen to know how old we were and how we were enjoying their country. But they were particularly curious to know which country we came from. Every person who blocked our path had the same question: 'You are coming from?' This was invariably followed by a monetary proposition.

Kevin got so fed up of this after a while that he decided to change his nationality. He was tired of being regarded as a walking sterling note. He was even tireder of everyone trying out the same few English phrases on him. I suggested that he tell them he was Swedish. But Kevin wasn't satisfied with being Swedish. Sweden wasn't half far away enough. With his luck, he'd be sure to bump into a succession of Indians who spoke fluent Swedish.

Instead, he began telling people that he came from the planet Mars. And when they didn't believe him, he started hopping up and down in the street, flailing his arms about in a vivid re-enactment of how he had descended to Kanchipuram from a spaceship. Crowds gathered to watch him. They had never seen a Martian before.

Kevin began to gain confidence, as one by one, beggars, tradesmen and rickshaw drivers bounced off the armour of his new-found origin. Then, just as he had approached the peak of his triumph, he was stopped in his tracks by an eager young 'businessman' who was determined to expose his fraud.

The conversation went something like this:

'Hello,' said the Indian.

'Hello!' replied Kevin.

'You are coming from?'

'Mars! I am coming from Mars!' (Kevin did a little jig, and simulated spaceship descent)

'You are coming from England.'

'No, I am coming from Mars. It's a different planet.'

'You are coming from *England!* You have English coins?'

'We don't have English coins on Mars.'

'You are going somewhere?'

'Yes, I am going somewhere.'

'Where are you going?'

'Somewhere.'

'I take you. I show you the way.'

'How can you show me the way? You don't know where I am going!'

'I take you. You have cigarette? Spare rupee?'

'What's a rupee? We don't have them on Mars.'

'You are needing dhobi? Clothes-clean? You want guide to temple?'

'We're allergic to temples on Mars. Go away.'

'Where is your room? I bring real English bread-butter to room. Yum, yum! Extra-strong bottle beer also!'

'You couldn't get in my room. It's a one-seater space shuttle.'

'Yes! I bring mosquito repellent your room! Also Japanese electric-element tea-maker!'

'No thanks. Push off.'

'You are needing anything?'

'No, I'm from Mars.'

'Ah! You can send me postcard from Mars? I am collecting stamps.'

'Oh, I give up.'

'You are from England?'

'Yes, you're too sharp for me. I am from England.'

'Ah! England! You know, I am M.A. Bachelor in English!'

'I kind of thought you might be. Say, have you ever been to Sweden?'

Deflated, Kevin's spirits only lifted again when we returned to the Kamakshiamon temple for the festival of the Golden Chariot. Every Tuesday and Friday, we had been told, the goddess Kamakshi (an incarnation of Parvati) was towed round the circumference of the temple grounds in a golden chariot to bless marriages. The rest of the week, Kamakshi's chariot took it easy in an old garage some way up the road.

The Indians seemed to take Kamakshi's blessing very seriously indeed. Few of them in this part of the world would have dreamed of getting married without it. On the occasion of our visit, an astonishing 25,000 people had come into town to pay their respects in the temple. The scene, when we arrived at 8pm, was like a Roman triumph – hordes of jostling, excited people crowding in through the narrow entrance to the courtyard within.

We had arrived just in time. Moments after we passed into the temple grounds, the crowd suddenly ceased its activity and a respectful silence descended. It was pitch black. Kevin and I peered at each other, wondering what we had let ourselves in for. Suddenly, from out of the gloom to our right, came the unmistakeable sound of an electric generator starting up. And then there was light. Kamakshi's processional chariot, previously only a dark, dim shadow, lit up in a blaze of neon-coloured bulbs.

What a sight it was! The entire carriage was plated with 24-carat gold and was festooned with bright flowers, garlands, taffeta and silk tassels. The tiny model of Kamakshi was completely buried in all this decoration. The solid gold figurines of her attendant deities and the two red and gold fairground horses ranged around her on the chariot, were brilliantly illuminated. A great howl of awed appreciation rose up from the crowd.

I had never seen a god propelled by a diesel tractor before. The carriage began to move slowly forward, followed by a troupe of musicians playing an eerie, hypnotic rhythm on squeezebox, horns and drums. An elderly fat priest forced his way up to me through the crowd, and gripped my arm. 'You *see?*' he proclaimed, his face radiant with joy. 'You see how wonderful is our *god?* You think that this is all *begging*. But it is *not* begging!' I tried to direct his attention to the growing crowd of acquisitive infants around us, all chanting 'Rajah! Master! You have pen? You have cigarette? You give rupees?', but he sprang away the next second – still crowing with ill-suppressed glee – without giving them a second glance.

The processional car stopped four times in all, once at each corner of the massive temple grounds. On each occasion, the two temple elephants heading the procession were drawn to a halt, and a succession of firecrackers and rockets were lit practically under their trunks. They appeared remarkably unmoved by all this commotion. It was impossible for Kevin and me to remain unmoved, however. The combined effect of the jostling, cheering crowds, the wailing, insistent ceremonial music, the smoke and smells of fireworks and incense, and the devilish features of the ghostly gopurams, shot into relief by the bright glow of Kamakshi's flaming chariot, was the most magical, mystical experience we had had in India to date.

A lot of the magic went out of it, however, when I caught sight of what the temple priest on top of the chariot itself was up to. Each time the car came to a stop, he would stretch his hand out to the multitudes below for their money. Most of them had by this time worked themselves up into such a trance of religious ecstasy, that they were prepared to give him the shirts off their backs. Many people were waving large fistfuls of banknotes in the air, desperate to get his attention. When he looked their way and took their cash, they were so grateful they kissed his feet and fell sobbing to the ground. After collecting everybody's money, the priest offered it to the Kamakshi figurine on the car behind him, waved a smoke-laden chasuble up and down in front of it, and told all the donors that their marriages had been blessed by Heaven. To conclude the ritual, he knocked a number of flaming incense-coals from the chasuble to the ground. Wherever the coals landed, the crowd fell to their knees groaning and paid them tearful, grateful homage. It was all very emotional.

January 26th

Today we made the acquaintance of Netaji. More accurately, he made the acquaintance of us. And once adopted by Netaji, we couldn't get rid of him. The moment we showed him the slightest interest, we became his parents, his brothers, his mentors and his best friends. This whole day revolved exclusively around Netaji. He would have liked nothing better, we concluded, than for the rest of our lives to revolve exclusively around Netaji. His desire for our friendship was so powerful and consuming, we couldn't comprehend it. Let alone reciprocate it.

Netaji first appeared early this morning. He came offering to take our clothes to a dhobi for washing. He returned an hour later with the clothes cleaned, and squatted down on Kevin's bed for a nice long chat. He remained there the rest of the morning. We learnt that he was seventeen years old (though he looked only twelve) and was still at school. What Netaji hadn't learnt at school simply wasn't worth knowing. He gave me the names of every cricketer in every English cricket team over the past ten years. Then he told me how much milk was produced in Sweden last year. Then he told me a whole host of 'interesting facts', such as how long it took to build the QE II and other famous ships.

As I listened to this incredible monologue (it went on for two hours without a single pause), I took stock of Netaji. On first impression, he looked like so many other Indian boys – with the usual shock of sleek black hair, the familiar grinning set of brilliant-white teeth, the eager, moist-brown eyes, the clear-skinned but hungry features, and the wiry, undernourished body. But then I noticed the deep scar tracing a jagged path down from his lip to the base of his chin. I asked him what had caused this. He replied that as an infant he had been sitting on the side of the road when a bullock-drawn haywain had passed by. The wheels of the cart had a vicious circle of sharp wire spokes fanning out from the axles. One of the spokes had caught his lip, and had raked the entire left side of his face open.

Netaji informed us that this accident had deprived him of

speech for over a year. Kevin and I exchanged a meaningful look. Could Netaji be making up for lost time? We gazed at him in dismay. Would his stream of inconsequential chatter ever come to a stop?

Netaji told us that today was Independence Day in India. He wanted to go somewhere to help us celebrate it. We tried to protest, but he wasn't to be denied.

'We go see temple!' he announced, his bared teeth gleaming in the light of the dim room's single bulb.

'No, Netaji! We've seen enough temples!' we protested. 'Why don't you go home?'

He shook his head. 'Parents away for weekend. I stay with you. We go to temple. We go to temple *now*.'

Kevin groaned and rolled his eyes. He was trying to decide which was worse: going round another boring temple, or spending the whole weekend with Netaji.

Actually, the Varatha Temple which he took us to was well worth the visit. The massive *rajagopuram* (temple tower) had just been renovated, and was most impressive. So was the wide, spacious Marriage Hall – supported by one hundred finely carved pillars – within. It looked out over a large ghat containing two small temples. 'Every twelve years god comes,' explained Netaji. 'He comes as animal, and each time he comes, new temple built in water tank.' I looked at the ghat, and did a rapid mental calculation. In another hundred years, there would be so many temples in there to commemorate Vishnu's visits that he wouldn't be able to come anymore.

Netaji asked us if we were hungry and then, without waiting for a response, ran off out of sight. He returned with three banana leaves full of what appeared to be a mush of greasy, bright yellow maggots. 'Sweets!' announced Netaji. 'Yum, yum!' He told us it was a mixture of lemon-rice, *ladau* (sugar) and onions. Kevin's face registered absolute disgust. Netaji didn't seem offended when we gave him our portions. He ate the lot, and thoroughly enjoyed it.

We had planned to lose Netaji outside the temple, but he had other plans. 'We go see film!' he said. '*English* film! You like!'

Actually, this didn't sound a bad idea at all, so we decided to string along. Off the bus back in Kanchipuram, Netaji sprinted off – with no warning – down a backstreet. We followed at a run. Neither of us had any idea why we were running. We were quite breathless by the time we caught up with him, having scurried down a bewildering warren of hidden lanes and narrow alleys. I clung onto Netaji, and demanded an explanation.

'We run quick! Friends no see, parents no find out!' he replied.

'Parents no find out *what?*' I quizzed him.

'Parents no find we go see *sex film!*' tittered Netaji.

We looked at him in alarm.

'Yes!' exulted Netaji, clapping his hands together in excitement. 'Sexy film! English sexy film! You like!'

Before we had a chance to protest, he had dragged us inside the nearby cinema and thrust us down into two empty seats. Then he ran off to another part of the dark interior and sat somewhere else. He apologised that this was necessary, since it wouldn't do for him to be recognised in such an establishment with two foreigners. Before leaving, he assured us that we would love this film. It was the most popular movie playing in town.

The film was called *Together With Love*. It wasn't a sex film at all, but an educational film for expectant mothers! The screen was alive with heavily pregnant ladies wallowing around doing exercises on the floor of a pre-natal classroom. Some sort of raucous American commentary was going on in the background. It was so loud as to be completely unintelligible. Kevin and I held our hands to our ears, and looked around at the audience in the cinema. They were all men. All we could see of them was rows of staring, excited eyes and grinning teeth. Everybody was riveted to the screen. The only times there was any reaction was when a naked female breast loomed onto the screen, and then a ripple of nervous, lascivious laughter swept through the audience. We were quite at a loss to understand this – all the breasts which came into view were heavily swollen with milk, and generally had a thirsty baby attached to them.

Kevin and I suffered twenty minutes of this curious spectacle, and then left the cinema. Netaji leapt out of his seat and followed us outside. On the walk back into town, we tried again and again to lose him down one or other of the numerous backstreets, but with no success. Whenever we thought we'd finally given him the slip, back he'd pop into sight laughing and skipping along about ten yards ahead of us. He never came any closer, and was never farther away. At this distance, he could both pretend he didn't know us (in case his friends or parents turned up) and yet be pretty sure of retaining his hold on our company. Netaji was a very sharp cookie indeed.

We did get rid of him in the end, though. Back at the lodge, Netaji got collared by five chums on the roof who wanted him to share a hash cigarette with them. This offer proved irresistible, Netaji's vigilance slipped for a moment, and we bolted thankfully out into the freedom of the streets.

Kevin now announced he was hungry and suggested we try a grubby old roadside restaurant. He asked the cook at the entrance for a cheese omelette. But the cook didn't know what a cheese omelette was. Kevin had to explain it to him. He explained it first by drawing a series of pictures illustrating what a cheese omelette looked like at each stage of its evolution, and then – when this failed to work – by grabbing some pots and pans and flailing them about in the air to suggest how to prepare it. From the other side of the street, it looked like he was sending semaphore messages to the cook.

Gradually, light dawned. The cook's face broke slowly into a fat, greasy smile of comprehension. Yes, he indicated, he would be delighted to prepare a cheese omelette for his honoured English guest. We sat down inside and waited. Two Indians from the other table silently rose from their seats and came across to wait with us. The waiter, his wife, and the cook's wife also appeared. They had come to wait with Kevin as well. A trickle of curious Indians started to come in off the street to watch. By the time Kevin's cheese omelette arrived some five minutes later there were eleven people waiting to see him eat it. Oh yes, and the cook. The cook was twisting his apron between his hands in an agony of suspense, waiting for Kevin's verdict on the omelette.

Kevin eyed the omelette warily. It had a suspect rubbery texture, but it certainly looked like a cheese omelette all right. He took a large forkful, chewed it twice and swallowed it. The next second, his eyes glazed over, his knees began trembling, and his face went quite red. The omelette had been laced with powerful green chillies. He downed the glass of water set out for him, and made to leave. Eleven pairs of eyes bore him down into his seat again. They wanted to see him enjoy his omelette. The cook, unable to control himself any further, waded across and leant heavily over Kevin, desperate to know how he was enjoying his omelette.

'Oh, fine, fine!' mumbled Kevin. 'Never tasted better...' He held up his hand, and waved his five outstretched fingers at the cook in a gesture of appreciation.

This was a bad mistake. The cook, overjoyed with his success, misinterpreted Kevin's gesture. He studied Kevin's five fingers waving in the air, and concluded that he must be ordering *five more omelettes*. What a compliment! Glowing with pride, he returned to his frying pan and starting selecting his choicest chilli peppers for Kevin's pleasure...

By the time Kevin had finished the first omelette, sweat was streaming down his suffused brow and he had completely lost the power of speech. But he had finished it. And he could just about summon a weak smile of appreciation to let his packed audience know what a pleasure it had been.

Imagine his surprise then when the second omelette arrived. The cook came over personally to serve it to him. It slid under his nose like a death sentence.

Kevin's face registered unmitigated horror. 'Take it away!' he tried to shout, but his voice was gone and nobody could understand him. The staff interpreted his wild protesting gestures as excited anticipation, and they hastened to assure him that all was well, that he would always be welcome here, and that indeed they would even set aside a special table for him each evening if that was his wish.

He shot me a mute, desperate look of appeal, but I couldn't help. Kevin plunged into the second omelette with the air of a man consigned to the gallows. More Indians came in off the street. Everybody was magnetised by the sight of a Westerner who enjoyed their cooking so much that he's ordered six omelettes at a single sitting. The cook looked at the tears of joy starting up in Kevin's eyes, and was so touched that he himself began to weep. It was a very emotional scene.

Kevin was only halfway through the second omelette when

the third one arrived. He stared at it as if it was Marley's Ghost. He stopped eating and looked over at the cook, who already had omelettes four and five on the go. A low moan drifted out of the side of Kevin's omelette-packed mouth. He upped from his seat, fought his way through the crowd of onlookers, and fled out into the street as fast as his legs would carry him. The cook tried to follow him down the road, holding a frying pan before him in a prayer of supplication, but Kevin never looked back.

I passed the cook on my way out. His face wore such a look of dejection that I told him Kevin had merely run off to tell his friends how good the omelettes were, and he would surely be back for more later.

January 28th

The next objective on our route was the 'temple city' of Madurai, which took us even nearer to the southern tip of the continent. We arrived in Madurai at 7am, after a gruelling ten-hour bus journey.

This bus was manned by the most reckless driver we had yet encountered. Minutes after screeching off into the dark night, he sent the bus flying over a giant pothole in the road. The whole vehicle, wheels spinning freely, flew into temporary orbit. The long road to Madurai was so poorly surfaced that it destroyed the bus's already weak suspension and left every passenger on board praying desperately for deliverance. Kevin and I spent the whole journey tightly gripping our seats to prevent being catapulted out of the windows.

Another interesting feature of this bus was that all the Indian parents on board had bedded their children down in the gangways. This meant every time we wanted to get off to relieve ourselves or to get a cup of cha, we had to engage in all sorts of athletic contortions to avoid stomping on some recumbent infant.

At Madurai bus station, we were surrounded by a squadron of rickshaw drivers clamouring to take us where we didn't want to go. We beat them off, and went in search of a restaurant for breakfast. Suddenly, a paan-chewing, bow-legged 'helper' appeared at our side and snatched up my bags. Off he went up the road, with Kevin and me giving furious chase. By the time we'd caught him up, he had booked us into three separate hotels and collected three separate amounts of commission from the proprietors. What an ingenious way of making money!

We booked into the New Modern Cafe hostel, just off Town Hall Road, and immediately went to view the Shree Meenakshi Temple. It was set within a large complex of its own – making it virtually a city within a city – and we found the high southern tower open for tourists to climb. Fighting our way to the top, along an increasingly narrow series of steps heavily populated with screeching bats, we came out into the open via a small trapdoor hatch. We squatted precariously on the tiny viewing ledge, looking down on a vast panorama of temple buildings, gopuram towers and ceremonial shrines below, and became increasingly uncomfortable. The view was superb, but there no safety barriers up here and we were rapidly overcome by vertigo.

Preparing to descend, I suddenly noticed a French hippy who had somehow crawled along the narrow summit ledge and wedged himself between two of the balustrades. Kevin wondered how he had had the nerve to get out there. I wondered how on earth he was going to get back. Especially as he seemed to be stoned out of his head on grass. As he began to pack yet another wedge into his chillum, he gave us a cheerful, languid wave of final farewell.

Coming out of the temple city, we walked into Madurai proper. It was, by Indian standards, a very clean and modern town. We had several approaches from salesmen offering ready-to-wear cotton suits and clothes, and we did have to be careful not to be mown down by the fleets of bicycles and mo-peds coming both ways down the narrow footways, but after Madras and Kanchipuram these were only minor inconven-iences. Madurai was far and away the most pleasant Indian city we had yet come across.

The evening was spent in the cinema, viewing a popular Hindi 'horror' film called *Purana Mandir.* It was an incredible epic – full of haunted houses, moonlit graveyards, hysterical women, deranged woodsmen, cackling witches, blood-streaked showers, gloomy mortuaries and lots of very bad weather in-deed. It rained and thundered and spat lightning for over an hour. Then, quite suddenly, the portly hero and heroine were transported to a haystack in the middle of a sunny beach. This was very odd.

What was even odder, however, was what occurred in the very next scene. In this, all the main protagonists were sud-denly whisked away from trying to murder each other in the old haunted house, and inexplicably set down in a modern strobe-lit discotheque. The audience gasped, and clapped in appreciation. What a brilliant piece of editing! But they hadn't seen anything yet. For onto the disco floor came tripping a gargantuan limbo-dancer in gold pantaloons. She had the most enormous pair of breasts, with gold tassels swinging from them. They looked like a couple of giant armour-plated wa-termelons. As they loomed up on the screen, everybody in the cinema recoiled in their seats. Then, as we watched, this mammarian *tour de force* began lunging around the disco floor, singing a gay little song. In the middle of this, she plucked a feeble little Indian chap off his seat, whipped off his cool Michael Jackson shades, and made him sing the gay little song too. As the dancer advanced on him, he began to say his prayers and prepared to be buffeted to death by those unbelievably dangerous breasts.

He was saved by the interval. So were we. The film had already run two hours, and we were too tired to stay for the second half. On the way out, just as we were commenting on the use of wired bats in the film's graveyards and haunted houses, a *real* bat entered the auditorium and began flitting eerily across the empty screen.

We made one last detour before returning home, to a local vegetable market. Here, a charming sloe-eyed local girl casually offered me her body, while Kevin went into loud raptures about coconuts. 'These coconuts are just the job!' he boomed down the market. 'I think I'll take some home with me! I reckon I could *live* on coconuts!' He emerged with five coconuts, and began bowling them down the dark, empty street in a vain attempt to break them open. Much later, in the silent still of the night, I could hear him at the other end of the corridor, bouncing the resilient coconuts off the walls of his room, and then furiously stamping on them. The way he cursed those coconuts, you'd think they'd break and yield their fruit just to keep him quiet. But they didn't. In the morning, he still had five intact coconuts.

January 29th

The five-hour bus journey from Madurai to KodaiKanal was the most perilous expedition we had yet undertaken. Indian buses are bad enough when they are travelling the straight and narrow, but when they start going up into mountain passes, you are never quite certain of reaching your destination alive.

The hill-station of KodaiKanal lies some 2,500 feet above sea level. In the days of the Raj, it was a favourite haunt of British officers eager to escape from the summer heat of the plains below. The tortuous ascent up narrow, winding and crumbling mountain roads left us wondering how any of them ever reached it.

The principal hazards on this dizzying ascent were not, however, the regular knife-edge bends and curves in the dust-track road, but the cautionary road signs. The most dangerous one had been stuck on the very edge of a diving precipice. 'Beware!' it stated. 'Distracting View!' Our driver was so distracted (by the sign, not the view) that he nearly plunged the bus off the cliff.

This peril passed, the rest of the journey up to Kodai was very pretty indeed. Particularly charming were the small rural villages along the route. The inhabitants themselves were simple people, with an inexhaustible supply of good humour and hospitality. They were not, however, above having a laugh at the expense of visiting tourists. At one village we stopped at, a party of smiling schoolboys appeared and began waving cheerily at us. It was only when we drew away that I noticed that every one of them had their trousers down. They had all been spraying the side of the bus!

Shortly after this 'water stop', we came to the top of the hill-range. The views from here were magnificent – wide, deep gorges, rushing waterfalls, thick forests of towering pines and rugged mountain crags. Reaching KodaiKanal itself, and booking ourselves into the Greenlands Youth Hostel in Koaker's Walk, we found ourselves overlooking the most spectacular views of all. Below the lodge, an unsurpassable panorama of mountains, valleys and plains stretched out before our eyes.

We gazed out upon this marvellous vista for some minutes, and then I broke our respectful silence by challenging Kevin to put his feelings about it into words. He pondered a moment, and then offered 'Nice!' When it comes to nature, Kevin can be awfully plebeian sometimes. He has no soul.

We found the Greenlands lodge very quiet and pleasant. The dormitory accommodation was very cheap (Rs7.50, or 50 pence, a night), it had good kitchen facilities, and the lovely little sun-veranda overlooked a pretty flower-border, verdant meadows and a series of calm mountain peaks. In stark contrast to the heat and dust of Madurai, the air was clear, fresh and very invigorating. It gave us the energy to go walking immediately after dropping our bags.

The small, bustling town of Kodai is full of amazing signs. First we were drawn into the Tibetan Brothers restaurant by an intriguing sign saying: 'Sir! Here enjoy Soup!' Then we came across another one which read: 'Indian Handy Crafts and Curious.' Finally, best of all, we saw the billboard for the Hotel Jai. This read: 'Be our COSY GUEST tonight, and WAKE UP GAY in the morning!'

I was just lazing by the side of Kodai's famous boating lake, watching parties of rich Indian tourists arrive (they came on Disco Buses, played Michael Jackson incessantly on their Walkmans, and greeted each other with loud Americanisms like 'Hey! My *man!*') when a local tout offered me some magic mushrooms. He gave me twelve tiny, wizened examples of this hallucinatory fungus, and told me I would see some very strange things. I told him I had already seen some pretty strange things, but took the mushrooms anyway. Nothing happened. Except that I later ended up in hysterics under a table at the Tibetan Brothers with a French girl who was trying to teach me goat-language. Jeanette spoke fluent goat. Back home in France, she was a goat-herder.

KodaiKanal had a large tourist population of hippies. They hung out generally at a place called Israel's, which is famous for its banana cake and custard. Everyone sat round on the floor of this dark 'restaurant' smoking cannabis, eating magic mushrooms and playing psychedelic music on Spanish guitars. Nobody spoke. They were all solid gone.

Time passed very slowly in Israel's. I returned to Greenlands convinced it was past midnight. It was actually only 9.30pm. I entered the lodge to find the landlord in heated argument with a Californian girl named Sunita. He had just given her a letter telling her, and her three fellow girl-travellers, to vacate the premises. They had apparently broken his 'rule' requiring them to be off the streets and back in the lodge by 9pm every night.

Sunita couldn't comprehend this rule. Her wide, independent features were set in an angry frown. She demanded that the landlord explain himself. But he was a retired colonel of the Indian army, and his squat walnut-brown face displayed an arrogant, patronising sneer which showed him unaccustomed to being opposed. Especially by women. The colonel had some very odd ideas about women. 'I am responsible man!' he declared hotly. 'You girls are like my daughters. Not proper you stay out late!'

Sunita's eyes rolled heavenward. 'I do not believe this!' she howled. Whereupon, I offered to arbitrate the dispute. The colonel's arguments were so ridiculous, however, that I was soon struggling to keep a straight face.

'What is cause for humour?' commanded the colonel, his dignity threatened. I pointed at Sunita, who had just seen the funny side of things and had vanished under the table, unable to contain her mirth.

The colonel decided the time had come to justify his position fully. He brought the conversation round to Napoleon Bonaparte. He was a big fan of Napoleon. And there was one particular speech of Napoleon's which he particularly favoured. He was determined to recite it to us.

'During this marathon period...' he began. But was interrupted by Sunita diving back under the table in hysterics. He shot her a black look, and started again.

'During this marathon period – Napoleon he is saying in speech given in 1942...'

But now I interrupted. 'Hold on!' I said. 'Napoleon wasn't around in 1942!'

The colonel fixed me with a steely gaze. 'During this marathon period, Napoleon is saying in *1942*...'

Again I protested. 'No, no! Not possible! Napoleon, he is *dead* in 1942. He is being dead for many, many years. How possible he is making speeches from six feet under?'

I now had a very angry colonel on my hands. 'You *know* Napoleon Bonaparte?' he enquired icily.

'Not personally,' I replied. This was enough for the colonel. He dismissed my objections without further ado.

'Ah! Precisely!' he said. '*During* this marathon period... (brief flash of eyes defying us to interrupt again)...I have given my blood, sweat and toil in reciprocity for the good of the nation!'

His marathon quotation finished at last, the colonel gave a

long sigh of relief.

'*That* is what Napoleon is saying in 1942, *that* is why I am feeling responsible, and *that* is why I am requesting you girls to be leaving!'

'What you mean,' summed up Sunita, 'is that you *request* us to leave, but if we don't obey this request, you'll kick us out anyway?'

'This is correct!' said the colonel, pleased at being understood. 'This is *reciprocity!'*

He was so grateful he'd got the message across that he followed me into the dormitory to shake my hand.

January 30th

Kevin and I arose at 5.30am to witness an awesome sunrise from the foot of the lodge. Wrapped in sleeping bags and blankets, we watched the sun blaze over the horizon like a fiery phoenix, illuminating the vast landscape below to a distance of some 60 kilometres. The previous day's clouds had settled on the mountain peaks like thick whipped cream. Driven up by the heat of the sun, the vaporous mist now rapidly disintegrated, breaking off into rolling streamers which gave the appearance of slow-motion waves smashing against the nearby cliffs.

We returned to the lodge and met Anthony, the cook. Anthony was a cheerful, grinning monkey of a man, another curious relic of the Raj, with appalling taste in clothes (he was wearing a purple-flowered shirt and a moth-eaten green jersey) but a superlative gift for cooking.

'What do you want for supper?' he addressed Kevin in perfect English.

'Well, what have you got?' replied Kevin, fully expecting a choice between *thali* and nothing else.

Anthony's head waggled furiously back and forth. 'No, no, *no!*' he protested. 'It is not a matter of what I have *got*. What do you *want?*'

Kevin's eyebrows soared with surprise; he gave the matter quick consideration. 'What I *want* is steak and kidney pud!' he decided. 'But I don't expect you...'

Anthony cut him short. 'I will make it!' he announced. 'I will also make lemon meringue pie.'

Kevin's mouth began to work agitatedly. 'With custard?' his voice quivered.

'Certainly with custard!' stated Anthony.

Tears of gratitude sprang into Kevin's eyes. He choked down a sob of emotion, and spent the rest of the day singing Anthony's praises.

To get Kevin's mind off supper, I took him off to play golf. Kodai has a very large and famous golf course. It is set on a series of undulating hills and forests, and is kept in constant peak condition. Which is odd, since hardly anybody comes here to play. Only in the single month of May, when the 300 or so club members roll up from all over India for the annual meet, is the course's vast potential fully exploited.

We had played just nine holes when thick banks of mountain mist rolled over the course, obscuring the herds of cows employed to keep the grass down and making further play impossible. Despite the fog, Kevin could still look back – on the walk home – on the incredible variety of different views Kodai had offered on the 7-kilometre outward journey. Here one can look out or on to magnificent cliffs and mountains, tranquil river, rushing waterfalls, rustic farm-scenes, charming cottages and churches, busy streets, wide sunlit lakes, and lush fields, meadows and parks. In amongst all this variety however, the unifying colour of Kodai is green – a deep, luscious, fecund green of peaceful serenity.

We returned to the Greenlands Lodge minutes before it too was claimed by the fog. Even as we crossed the veranda, eerie, ectoplasmic fingers of swirling mist clutched at our ankles before prising their way under door and window frames and penetrating the building itself. The temperature fell rapidly. It became very cold.

Kevin tried fruitlessly to light a stack of green logs in the fireplace. The handyman passed him a can of kerosene, neglecting to tell him what was in it. Kevin cheerfully heaved half a can of the stuff into the struggling fire. The blinding blowback of flame which resulted instantly singed his virgin beard back to stubble again. He only recovered from the shock when Anthony produced supper. And what a supper it was! Steak and kidney pie, with mashed potatoes and green beans! Followed by a delicious banana custard. Everybody at the table was so overcome by this unexpected feast that conversation, for much of the rest of the evening, was desultory and quiet. Full stomachs and satiated appetites drove us all shortly to our beds.

January 31st

Returning from an enjoyable hour boating on Kodai's beautiful lake, I ran into Sunita, Jeanette and the other two girls in their party. They had finally been ejected from Greenlands by the colonel. They were all sitting on a low knoll on the roadside, eating magic mushrooms. A local monkey on an empty leash joined the company, and attached itself to Jeanette. First it savaged her rucksack, and then it vanished down the front of her T-shirt. A lively mongrel, drawn by this activity, also tried to climb down the front of her T-shirt. The monkey clambered out, and jumped up and down on Jeanette's head while the dog swung back and forth on her shoulders, trying to get at it.

Two young Indian men appeared. They were also very interested in her T-shirt, or rather in what lay beneath it. The liberated, independent behaviour of Western women in this country attracts a lot of salacious interest from Indian men – many of them seem to expect young female tourists to leap into bed with them at the drop of a hat. This particular couple must have been in their early to mid 30s, but were giggling and pointing furtively at Jeanette like a pair of schoolboys. One of them finally sidled up to her. He put his hand in his pocket, and withdrew...a contraceptive sheath. He waved the limp rubber right under her nose, and announced loudly: 'I wonder where I'll get to put *this?*' Jeanette told him.

Supper tonight was steak and kidney pie again, followed by rhubarb crumble. Andrew, Kevin and I gave Anthony a rousing cheer after we had finished. He had been standing next to us, wearing a proud, proprietary air and a bizarre shirt (this one had luminous orange and green roses growing all over it) throughout the entire meal, anxiously awaiting a verdict.

Kevin then enlivened proceedings by wearing his new hat. It looked like a dead racoon. Andrew and I told him it was hideous, but the Indians liked it. It had a soft, furry brown border and a little black fur bobble which they found irresistible. The handyman, Anthony and even the colonel, took turns to slip up behind Kevin and lovingly stroke it. The resident cat was ignored all evening. Later on, when all was quiet and Kevin had gone to bed, the cat snuck on the hat and jealously pissed in it.

February 1st

The new month started on a very cold note. It was absolutely freezing, and everyone was huddled round the only warm spot in the lodge – Anthony's cooking stove. The colonel was doing a roaring trade, hiring out extra blankets at a rupee apiece. They were all ex-army issue.

Over breakfast I met Sally, an English girl, who was still recovering from her experience on a train coming into Delhi a few weeks back, in the wake of Mrs Gandhi's assassination by the Sikhs. Ten miles north of the city, a mob of angry Hindus had stopped the train, boarded it, dragged every Sikh passenger (about 200 in all) outside, and promptly beheaded every one of them by the side of the rails, while Sally looked on in horror.

The cold blanket of mist had buried the lodge completely by the time we had taken breakfast. The damp, chill air didn't agree with me at all. I retired to my bunk with a slight fever. So did Kevin. He had the same fever, but with the added complication of diarrhoea. Both of us sat around miserably this evening watching the others tuck into Anthony's speciality dish of the day – steak and chips, followed by lemon meringue pie. We were too ill to eat any of it. Kevin took off his furry hat in mourning for his lost meal, and made to weep into it. That was when he discovered what the cat had done in it last night.

February 2nd

When we woke this morning, I was feeling a good deal better and Kevin a good deal worse. He managed to struggle out of bed, but then, on every occasion that I turned to say something to him, he had vanished into the toilet. I took a brief look out of the window to check the weather: it was still damp, misty and cold, and looked like staying so for the rest of the day. I therefore made the decision that, for the good of our health, we should return to Madurai without delay.

We took the bus down to the hot, dry plains again in the company of Sunita (who had never quite managed to achieve 'reciprocity' with the colonel) and with a quiet, wry-humoured Dutch girl called Maryke. The journey was once again very bumpy and dangerous. The only light relief came from the bus's ticket collector, with his periodic cries of: 'We stop now! Five minutes for tea and urine!'

Back in the heat and dust of Madurai, I collapsed back into the New Modern Cafe, while Kevin took Maryke off to tour the Shree Meenakshi Temple. The three of us met up again for supper at the Amutham restaurant, which had the following proud boast on its menu cover:

It is the mythological belief that Devas and Asuras churned the ocean of Milk using a big hill as the churner and a huge snake as the rope to get AMBROSIA. Amutham Restaurant has derived the idea from this to leave no stone unturned to produce delicious and wholesome food just for you.

An admirable sentiment, this, but my BOEING 747 SANDAE still took an hour to arrive. And this dessert came before – not after – my main dish of SLICKED CHICKEN AND VEGETABLES. Though neither Kevin nor I had much appetite tonight. Maryke had been telling us where Anthony had got the meat for his steak and kidney pies. It explained why we'd seen so few stray dogs in Kodai.

Later that night, as Maryke and I whispered away about Indian philosophy in the privacy of her room, there was a strange, shuffling sound outside the door. Then something was slid under it.

It was one of Kevin's ninety-two contraceptives.

February 3rd

We started the day by trying to book bus tickets for Kanya Kumari (the southern tip of India) in Madurai's chaotic bus station. This was a remarkably complicated procedure. Things went wrong from the start, with us being directed to the wrong reservation counter and buying two tickets for the wrong bus.

Discovering our mistake, we went to the right reservation counter and tried to buy two tickets on the right bus. We were told that we should have to cancel the two wrong tickets first. Well, that sounded reasonable, but then we were sent away to a special 'cancellation counter', which sent us away to a special 'cancellation *form* counter'. Well, we filled out our cancellation forms, returned them to the cancellation counter, went back to the reservation counter, and at last had our cancelled ticket money reimbursed. But then we were sent away again, to another counter which issued 'reservation *forms*, before being allowed to come back to the reservation counter and obtain our desired tickets for tomorrow's bus.

Kevin was feeling much better today. I knew he was feeling better, because his appetite had returned. Immediately we'd got the bus tickets, he dragged me into the nearby Taj Restaurant, intent on eating large helpings of food.

'What can you offer me that's *quick?*' he collared the waiter.

'*Everything* is quick!' came the grinning reply.

'Okay,' persisted Kevin. 'But what have you got that's

quicker than anything *else?'*

The waiter considered a moment, and then replied 'Chips.'

'Oh, that's fine!' exulted Kevin. 'I'll have two plates!'

The waiter went away. Ten minutes later, he returned.

'Oh good,' chortled Kevin expectantly. 'Here come my chips!'

But they weren't chips at all. The waiter had brought him two large plates of soggy potato *crisps*.

To stop Kevin assaulting the waiter, I whisked him and Maryke off to the Thirumalai Naick Palace. It was closed. On the walk home however, proceedings became lively when a record crowd of twenty-three local Indians gathered to watch us have a cup of tea. They wore a uniformly blank look of curiosity. To cheer them up, I gave them a spirited rendition of several jolly English music-hall songs (the Lambeth Walk, the Hokey-Cokey etc) but their faces remained just as blank as before. Even when Kevin went round with the hat for a collection, there was no change. They continued to stand there and stare like a row of waxwork dummies.

It was Kevin who finally startled the silent assembly out of their trance. He suddenly leapt up and bolted over to an old man sipping his tea nearby. Seizing the astonished geriatric's shaven pate in both hands, he began joyfully massaging it.

'This guy's got a head just like my father's!' he cried. And to prove the resemblance, he jammed a photo of his paternal relative under the confused old Indian's nose. Light dawned, and the aged sage broke into an excited stream of chatter. As the photo of Kevin's dad quickly passed round the crowd, the awful silence was broken and we were unexpectedly surrounded by a sea of smiling, laughing faces.

'My father's got a head just like yours!' Kevin stated with triumphant finality, and all the Indians nodded eager agreement. We had just made twenty-four new friends.

But Kevin had only just started. Today saw his star rocket to the highest point in the Indian firmament.

It all began when we travelled to the Mahdu cinema, six kilometres out of Madurai, to see James Bond in *Never Say Never Again*. Moments after climbing out of our rickshaw, Kevin suddenly discovered that he was a film star. Hordes of shouting, cheering men, women and children were flocking from miles around to see and touch him. The reason for this? Well, they all thought he was Sean Connery.

There were billboards all over town with the red, bloated, sardonic and generally dangerous features of Sean Connery painted on them (for this is how he is depicted on Indian film posters!) and the crowd instantly decided Kevin's features were identical. Their mistake was quite excusable. Kevin had just been overcharged (again) by a rickshaw driver, and had disembarked looking a dead ringer for Sean Connery. His face was red, it was bloated with rage, its lip was curled back in an ugly sneer, and his right eyebrow was raised in cynical contempt.

It was exactly the same 'look' worn by the film-poster Sean Connery. That 'look' was known to everyone in town, and here was an Englishman who had it off to perfection! There was no doubt about it: this Kevin must *be* Sean Connery!

As he was slowly sucked into a swirling whirlpool of adoring Indians – all of them insisting he shake their hands or bless their babies – Kevin gave a surprised shriek of alarm. Then he was completely lost to sight until, long minutes later, he was hauled free of the jostling masses by the rickshaw driver. He sat Kevin down, and asked him if he would like to go home now. Kevin shook his head weakly, and said that all he wanted to do right now was take a leak somewhere, and quick.

The rickshaw driver obligingly pointed him to a dark slit-trench on the side of the road, and Kevin stumbled gratefully off to it. But it wasn't his lucky night. No sooner had he unzipped his trousers in the dark ditch, than a large rat leapt out at him and nearly seized his assets. Running back out into the road in a state of terror, he was once more engulfed by the crowds.

Word of the Second Coming of Sean Connery had now reached the cinema itself. Consequently, as soon as Kevin appeared, everyone in the ticket queue stopped staring at Maryke (because she was an unaccompanied Western woman) and swivelled round to gaze wonderingly upon him. Not content with this, they began climbing over the ticket barriers to stand next to him, and a near-riot ensued. Finally, a bodyguard of sympathetic Indians formed around him, and he was ushered up to a private 'box' in the upper circle without further harassment. Here, he gave a long sigh of relief and lay back in his seat, thinking his ordeal over.

But it wasn't. One determined fan had slid past the bodyguard and into our box. He crept up silently, and slipped into the seat next to Kevin. Hardly able to credit his good fortune, this sallow-faced little man nuzzled contentedly into Kevin's shoulder, staring at him with unashamed adoration. Kevin gazed back with a look of undisguised horror.

Maryke and I spent the whole of the film fighting a losing battle against fleas and sleeplessness. Kevin, however, spent the whole of the film fighting off the affectionate Indian. He moved his seat three times to escape his devoted slave, but it was no good. The little man followed on doggedly on each occasion, collapsing back onto Kevin's shoulder after each move. Kevin made us repeated desperate requests for assistance. But we couldn't do anything. If this was the price of fame, we told him, he would simply have to learn to live with it.

February 4th

'What I want is a cheese sandwich!' groaned Kevin as he fell out of bed this morning. 'I'd give *anything* for a cheese sandwich!' I tried to keep him happy with a bar of chocolate, but it was white and mouldy with age and he immediately returned to inventing imaginary English breakfasts, with cheese sandwiches topping the bill.

We had not eaten properly for days. The intense heat, and the often greasy Indian food, had combined to rob us of our appetites. The restaurants' menus did not help matters. Take the Hotel Kannimara, where we had breakfast, for instance. Just one look at the menu – offering such unsavoury-sounding dishes as BOILER EGG, CASTARD, TRUTY FRUITS and (worst of all) BRAIN OMELETTE – and we were off our food for the rest of the day. The final straw came when a two-inch cockroach scuttled out of the restaurant sink and dived happily into my stuffed paratha.

Giddy with hunger, I spent most of breakfast with my head between my knees, as I waited for my brain to start working again. The only thing that got me moving at last was the cockroach falling off my plate and down the back of my neck.

Today we visited Thirupparankundram Temple, eight kilometres south of Madurai Junction. Stepping inside this temple –which is built into the mountainside and surmounted by a huge wicker tower with smoky 'prayers' to Shiva drifting out – is like travelling back a millennium in time. The massive central hall resounds with the mystic intonations of priests, the devotional prayers of the faithful, and the hollow boom and echo of massive drums and bells calling all present to the innermost shrine.

The place was packed with Indian families, each member bearing tiny bowls of coconut, fruit, vegetables and incense. Each bowl was lit by a very small, flickering oil-lamp. When the bells summoned all to prayer, the head of each family broke the coconuts and waited till all the milk had run to the ground. Then he or she opened small packages of grey and red powder, and smeared the marks of Shiva into each person's forehead, right down to the youngest infant. Later, their devotions completed, the family would come down to the temple ghat, purchase a small bag of boiled rice apiece, and cast it into the water as an offering to Shiva. The waters here frothed and foamed, as masses of tiny leaping fish rose to the surface to devour the rice donations.

The bus back to Madurai was packed solid. We stood in the crush for a while, then two seats became vacant. We had these for a minute or two, then surrendered them to two Indian ladies. Seeing this, two Indian men insisted we take *their* seats. Kevin found himself next to a young Indian girl, whose embarrassment at sitting next to a foreign man sent her into a fit of giggles. A few minutes of this, and Kevin was out of his seat again. He was immediately offered another seat, courtesy of another polite local, but this new berth left him crushed under an entire Indian family, so he crawled over to share my seat. For a few moments, all was now well. But then we discovered we were sitting on a nest of ants and fled the bus altogether.

February 5th

After saying goodbye to Maryke (who sadly had to go north) we took the night bus out of Madurai and travelled south to Kanya Kumari. The six-hour bus journey was pleasant enough, but we only achieved a minimum of sleep. Hence, by the time we booked into the Lekshmi Tourist Home at dawn, we were dog tired. Also, we hadn't eaten a solid meal for five consecutive days. Both of us therefore woke after a four-hour nap feeling even more horrible than when we had retired. Our limbs felt like water, and our stomachs were groaning from lack of food.

Dragging ourselves from our beds, Kevin and I shambled into town like two walking cadavers. Our eyes were haggard, our faces pinched and pale, our hands swinging uselessly at our sides, our jaws hanging slack and open, our whole bodies crying out for food and rest. People crossed the road to avoid us. Even beggars left us alone. Many of them backed off into doorways, or averted their eyes in superstitious fear.

We reached the end of the so-called high street (nothing more than an extended dirt-track) having seen no food-houses whatsoever. I clutched weakly at the shirt of a passing French traveller, and croaked: 'Restaurant...where is *restaurant?*' But he just gave me a blank look and replied: 'Restaurants? There *are* no restaurants in Kanya Kumari!'

Despondent, we fell into a nearby cha-house. The most sustaining fare on sale here was Horlicks. I spotted a tin of the nourishing beverage sitting on a high shelf. It was rusty and dented, and evidently hadn't been taken down for years. But I decided to chance it anyway. Five minutes later, my Horlicks arrived. It was totally undrinkable. The cha-man had made it with cold water.

69

The only good news we got today came from Andrew, who had followed us down from Kodai. He told us that we had narrowly escaped death. The bus which left Kodai for Madurai on February 3rd – i.e. the bus we *would* have caught had not Kevin's stomach pulled us out a day early – had plunged off the cliffs, leaving fourteen passengers dead and the rest severely injured.

Andrew then demonstrated the highest proof of friendship, guiding us to the only place in town which served food we could actually eat. Of course, it was just *thali* and chapatis, but in our starved state we devoured it with eager relish. We now understood how it was that so many long-stay travellers in India went into raptures over *thalis!*

Andrew shook his close-cropped head in puzzlement when I asked him his future plans.

'You know something?' he remarked. 'I've been right round the South-East Asia circuit now. I've been to Sri Lanka, to Thailand, to Burma and every other damn place – and I've found all these places pretty much alike and very easy to get to grips with. But India! I've been here over a month already, and I'm still no nearer to understanding it than when I first arrived! I expect I'll have to hang around until I *do* understand it...'

With the approach of dusk, we came to the viewpoint by the shoreline. Here masses of Indian tourists had gathered to see the sun set and the moon rise at the same time. Well, it didn't happen. The cloud on the horizon was a thick blanket, and the sun retired to bed beneath it long before it was due to set. We went off, only mildly disappointed, to a coffee bar which sold cashew nuts. I've always had a weakness for cashew nuts. But these were inedible, being very soggy and very bitter. I washed the taste away with our only good purchase of the day – a delicious fresh pineapple.

Kevin was still going on about cheese sandwiches today. The only time he stopped talking about them was when a dog-sized rat scampered down the main street and dodged between his ankles on its way back to cover.

February 6th

After a restless night tossing and turning beneath the powerful glow of the Full Moon, Kevin woke me to view the sunrise from the lodge rooftop. Spectacular though this was – the huge orange orb of the sun bursting over the 'three seas' of this southern tip of India (Bay of Bengal, Arabian Sea and Indian Ocean) – it wasn't half as fascinating as the activity on the other hotel rooftops around us. These were packed to capacity with wildly gesticulating Indian tourists, all swivelling back and forth to take in the rare sight of the sun rising and moon setting at one and the same time. As the spectacle achieved its maximum point of beauty, they all commenced hacking and spitting their approval, then began shouting a running commentary across to each other from one rooftop to the next.

Putting this pandemonium out of mind, I concentrated instead on the more restful sounds of the morning – the hypnotic chant of the Muslim mueddins, the calm drone of prayers drifting over from the nearby Catholic church, the sleepy chatter and clatter of the village folk below coming awake, and the slowly diminishing conversation of fishermen putting out to sea in small dhow-type boats for the morning catch.

Walking out, we discovered – just a few hundred yards away from the busy tourist precinct – the native part of town. This was a complete contrast to where we had just come from. Here dwelt a small community of fisher-folk living in plain, simple huts of mud, thatch and wood, carrying on their lives in much the same way that they had for many hundreds of years. It was completely unspoilt and untouched by the nearby commercialism of Kanya Kumari proper. The local villagers, dressed mostly in ragged dresses and loincloths (or nothing at all) greeted us with warmth tinged with surprise. They evidently didn't see many tourists. A group of naked, aboriginal fishermen beckoned us over to help them push their long boats (just three 20-foot planks lashed together) out to sea – their way of telling us we were welcome, I suppose.

The sea here was rough, most unsuitable for swimming. But the coast itself was beautiful – the sand was as smooth as silk, the palm trees were lush and green, and the sun was warm and mild, gently easing the tension of travel out of our necks and shoulders with tender, caressing fingers. We spent the rest of the day playing cards with some local children on the beach. They cheated abominably.

February 7th

I found Andrew and Kevin waiting outside the lodge this morning. They were studying a strange four-eared pig which was sleeping under a truck. I suggested we go out sailing, and they jumped at the idea. So we went back down to the fishing village in search of a boat.

Along the way, we dropped into the 16th century Catholic church, and found a marriage in progress. It was a very unusual marriage. To start with, the church didn't have any seats or pews and all the wedding guests were sitting or squatting on the bare floor. All their children, meanwhile, had torn their clothes off and were romping nakedly round the altar rail. Ignoring this, the officiating priest went through the ceremony supervised by a massive neon-lit statue of the Virgin Mary, which beamed down benevolently on him from its perch above the altar.

We found a party of fishermen on the beach willing to take us out in their boat for twenty rupees. The long, wide canoe they owned comprised five large tree-trunks welded together with pitch and tar. As soon as it had breasted the incoming tide, as soon as the large triangular canvas sail (mounted on a lone spar) had been set aloft, and as soon as we had seated ourselves precariously on the damp side-beams, the crew of pirates bombarded us with requests of cigarettes pens, spare rupees and English coins. They also wanted their photograph taken. Then they insisted that we take turns steering the boat. This, despite the uncertainty of balancing at the back of the vessel with only a thin tiller to hold onto, was actually a very enjoyable experience. And the view of the mainland of southern India from a mile or so out of sea was quite magnificent.

The grinning sailors let us catch a few fish each with their strong nylon lines, and then their demands for more money became pressing. They showed no signs of returning to land. Andrew didn't expect to get back at all. 'Well,' he remarked cheerfully. 'This is one way of getting to Sri Lanka!' As for Kevin, he wasn't deterred in the least. He loves the sea, does Kevin.

I tried to distract the fishermen from their financial demands by taking an interest in the necklace brooches they were wearing. Each small locket had a tiny picture of Jesus or the Virgin Mary in it. Of course, they misconstrued my interest completely. They thought I wanted to *buy* their devotional objects. In fact, they were so sure of making a sale here that they turned the craft homeward. We cruised in through a series of deadly shore-reefs and back onto the beach, with two of the crew daubing my sun-tan cream on their faces like war-paint and the other two trying to sell me Jesus. This aside, the outing had been a great success. Kevin wouldn't let me hear the end of it. For the time being at least, I heard nothing more about cheese sandwiches.

Part Two

Mowgli and the Wild West

February 8th

Today we went back north, and as we waited for the 6.30am bus to Kovalum, Kevin went back to the subject of English breakfasts. His preoccupation with food was approaching its climax.

It was indeed odd, I reflected, how the subject of food (particularly English food) was coming to dominate our thoughts and to assume such disproportionate influence on our conversations. But who could blame us? After all, we hadn't eaten a good, solid meal (discounting yesterday's *thali*) for over a week. And the strain was beginning to tell. Both of us looked forward to Kovalum (an apparent oasis of good grub) with the desperation of exiles awaiting repatriation.

The bus passed through Trivandrum, a noisy town with only one memorable road-sign (the ASIAN TOOLS AND GUILT CENTRE), before coming at last to Kovalum Beach at 10am.

Kevin, who had spent the entire journey in morose silence, immediately sprang out of the bus. He had seen a restaurant a mile back up the road. He swept aside the little Indian who had appeared to offer him accommodation with single-minded contempt.

'I don't want a room!' he mumbled, striding purposefully in the direction of food. 'What I want is *breakfast!*'

The diminutive guide gave chase, and told him this restaurant was closed. He introduced himself as Babu, and led the darkly muttering Kevin to the Moon Restaurant, which was open.

'Right!' Kevin addressed the waiter here. 'What I want to know is, do you have *chips?*'

The waiter recoiled in surprise, then recovered his poise. He nodded. Kevin gave a short grunt of appeasement. Scanning the menu rapidly (and ignoring curious items such as POTATO-ONIONFRIED and LEMON SOD) he gave the waiter the following directive:

'Okay, I'll start with cheese and tomato toast – make that *four* portions – and then...an omelette...and to follow...mmmm...yes, why not, *another* omelette, this time with cheese – lots of it – and tomato. And two plates of chips. Got that? *Chips*, not bloody potato crisps!'

The waiter stared at him dumbfounded and enquired what order he wanted his food served in.

'Oh, it doesn't matter what comes first,' declared Kevin. 'I don't care. And see if you can slip a banana pancake – oh, and a chocolate one – in there somewhere, there's a good fellow!'

The waiter turned to go, but Kevin pulled him back.

'One more thing,' he growled. 'While I'm waiting for my food, and I *do* hope that won't be long, I'll have a whole pot of tea *all to myself!*'

Kevin's mad cackle of hunger as he finished rolling off this formidable order drew cautious, wary glances from every other guest in the restaurant. His own eyes, however, were fixed with a dangerous piggy gleam on the back of the retreating waiter. And his jaws were now champing uncontrollably with the imminent prospect of breakfast.

When it arrived, Kevin swept the whole table clear for all

the dishes, and ate for a solid half-hour without raising his head once or uttering a syllable. Then, his repast completed, he sat back with a look of total satiation on his ruddy features. What a transformation some good food had achieved! Before the meal, his pale mask of tragedy suggested the acute suffering of one who has just lost a near relative. Now, however, he was back on top of the world again. He was so happy, he ordered another omelette.

Babu, the guide, went out of his way to get us placed in good accommodation. He was a smiley, carefree soul, dressed in a shiny green lunghi and a gay, flowery shirt, and he spoke perfect English. Right at the end of the beach, close to Kovalum's lighthouse, he found us a charming chalet bungalow for just Rs25 (£2) each. The rooms were bright and clean, and they had things one generally never sees in cheaper Indian lodges. Things like bowl-toilets, hand basins, writing tables, air-conditioning fans that worked and even waste-paper bins. Just as we were moving in, we ran once more into our good friend Andrew. He had arrived yesterday. As before, he was travelling one step ahead of us.

Kovalum Beach is a favourite haunt of hippies and junkies. Like Goa, further up the coast, people come here not just for the beautiful sun and beaches, but for the freely available (and very cheap) grass, hashish and harder drugs. One English traveller I spoke to was a trainee accountant in London. Every summer he came to India for six weeks. He started off at Anjuna Beach in Goa, getting a tan and spending all day at 'acid parties', then moved down to Kovalum for a couple of weeks to ingest plentiful quantities of the famous 'Kerala grass', then staggered back to Goa for a final leg of mind-blowing drug orgies. By the time they scraped him off the sand and put him back on his plane at Bombay, he was no better than a grinning idiot. The only reason he came back each year was that he simply couldn't remember anything that happened the year before.

On Kovalum beach, all the male tourists find themselves continually approached by shapely Indian women wearing fruit baskets on their heads. They sell pineapples, papayas, jam-fruit, bananas and mangoes at ridiculously cheap prices. All the female sun-worshippers, on the other hand, are surrounded as they lie topless on the beach by hordes of silent, staring Indian men who come specifically to Kovalum to gaze at bare breasts. The only two redeeming features of Kovalum are the excellent restaurants which are dotted all along the main beach complex, and of course the sea, which is calm, warm and quite excellent for swimming – and for snorkelling.

We spent most of the day on the beach or in the water. This evening we waited two hours in a restaurant for supper. Everything here proceeds at an abnormally slow, laid-back pace. We ended up sending Kevin into the kitchen to see if the cook was asleep or dead, and with instructions to murder him if neither excuse applied. He returned with three steaming bowls of cheese and tomato spaghetti, heavily laced with onions and whole garlic cloves. The cook was pardoned forthwith.

February 9th

I returned from snorkelling today to find that Kevin had acquired some tasteful company. A naked girl with very vital statistics had taken up position on the sand right next to him.

Poor Kevin. All thoughts of sun, sea and rolling surf went right out of his head. All he could think of now were those ninety-one contraceptives going to waste in his rucksack. He tried hard to relax, yet every few minutes or so his eyes would swivel round helplessly to gaze on the buxom beauty sleeping at his side He was particularly fascinated by the small bright ring of red pimples on her fulsome bare buttocks. And as the day progressed, this innocent fascination developed into a full-blown passion.

Eventually, Kevin's mouth was flapping open and shut like a distressed clam, with a series of low, unhappy moans drifting out of the side of it. The girl sat up briefly to ask him if he was in pain. All that he could think of in reply was that he had just been stung by a manta ray. 'Oh,' said the girl, and went back to sleep.

But if today presented Kevin with problems, they were as nothing compared to my own. This evening, waiting for our supper of GREENPEACE MASALA, Andrew and I became bored and tried some of the famous 'Kerala Grass' to see what was so wonderful about it. There was nothing wonderful about it at all. I spent the next four hours rooted to the sand outside the restaurant trying to claw my way back out of a bottomless chasm of blackest despair. Most of this time, also, I was sur-rounded by a hungry pack of wild dogs, who sat around me in a large circle waiting for me to peg out. Kevin came to collect me at midnight, and told me that Andrew and I had been given a dangerous hallucinogenic called 'angel dust' in with the grass. Now I understood why so many tourists lay around the beaches of Kovalum looking blank and destroyed.

February 10th

I woke up this morning very grateful to be alive. Last night's experience now seemed just a particularly bad dream. To forget it completely, I walked with Kevin down to the fishing village a few kilometres beyond the tourist beaches. We came to it via a beautiful Mughul mosque (built very much in the style of the Taj Mahal) which jutted out to sea on a rock promontory. Passing this, we were suddenly enveloped by a flock of small, dirty children chanting: 'Peanuts? Pineapple? Papaya? Coconut? Sea-shell? You have school-pen?' They all looked extremely pleased to see us.

The rustic fishing village of Kovalum was very similar to that of Kanya Kumari, though its beach was a good deal dirtier. The coastline was dotted with small piles of human turds waiting to be carried out to sea by the next tide. As we picked our way carefully through this minefield of excrement, some local fishermen spotted us. Again, as at Kanya Kumari, they accepted us into their village by enlisting our aid. On this occasion, we were required to help them pull in a catch of fish. Twenty minutes later, however, and with no sign of the catch getting any closer to land, we abandoned our positions on the thick rope line and headed on up the beach.

Returning to Kovalum proper, we bumped into Andrew. He looked like a walking wraith. 'I'm still stoned out of my head!' he groaned miserably. So we hauled him down to the beach, and let the sun and sea soothe away his cares. Later, however, we ended up at the Walk-In Restaurant on the beach, where the menu (MASALA DOSE, BOILED GRAB, BANANA SANE WITCHES and SCROMBIED EGGS) made him feel ill all over again.

February 11th

The lodge's small laundry-girl appeared early this morning.

She rapped insistently on my window, and peered in.

'Hello!' she called. 'You want peanuts? You taste. It is good!'

'No thanks,' I shook my head. 'They're all black.'

The smutty little urchin climbed through the window. 'You are giving me present?' she asked. 'Who invited you in?' I replied. She crowded me into the wall. 'Yes! You are giving – please – present!' I tried to ask her what for, but she continued: 'Gimme one book. One book. Gimme-one-book-one-book-gimme-one-book! You are giving *present!*' I ordered her to go away. 'Later, you gimme book?' she eased off slightly. '...later? You gimme book?'

She was just about to finally leave when her friend arrived. Her friend was even more persistent than she was. 'Hello!' announced the friend, also climbing into the room through the window. 'You gimme *pen?* Gimme-pen-just-one-pen-one-pen-gimme-pen!'

'Where the hell did *you* come from?' I enquired. She drew her brows together in a determined grimace. 'YOU GIMME PEN!' she shouted. 'No gimme pen!' I concluded firmly. 'Just gimme peanuts, and push off!'

They both went out the same way they'd come in – through the window.

The girls returned at noon, just as we were moving out. They gave me a card for our lodge which read: 'Hotel Holiday Home – If you stay here, you *fell* away from home.' Then they gave me a massive jack-fruit which seeped juice all over the bus going back to Trivandrum.

Not only was this particular bus packed to capacity to start with, but it stopped shortly to cram in an additional thirty-three schoolchildren. I spent the rest of the trip with a startled-looking child spread-eagled over my knees, listening to Andrew interrogating an Indian schoolmaster about tapioca plants.

Trivandrum bus station was a scene of absolute chaos. It was full of passengers sending out search parties for buses which seemed to turn up wherever and whenever they felt like it. The information desk was submerged with enquiries from panic-stricken travellers. And most people we saw were running blindly from one packed bus-rank to the next – or, more commonly, just standing in the middle of the mayhem looking stunned and lost.

We ourselves had just given up all hope of progress when, quite unexpectedly, the bus to Quilon turned up, exactly where we were standing. Two hours later, we were at our destination and had retired to our rooms in the Tourist Rest Home, ready to explore Kerala's inland waterways early the next morning.

February 12th

The eight-hour boat trip from Quilon to Allepey is one of the most beautiful and enjoyable experiences the foreign traveller can have in all India.

Sitting 'up top' involved a customary payment of two rupees each to the tiny, bird-like crew member on the boat's roof. His name was Hassan, and he wore a constant manic smile. I climbed up to meet him along with Sandra, a young Bavarian girl who was heading towards Calcutta to work in Mother Teresa's mission for handicapped children. As the trip progressed, Hassan took a real shine to the two of us. He kept up a non-stop monologue about his family, pausing occasionally to throw his arms around us, to dip into our cigarette packets, to fondle our necks and heads, or to jig up and down on the roof with my cassette headphones blasting big band music down his jug-like ears. Most of the rest of the time, however, he was busy harassing a group of intransigent Americans who refused to pay his tiny *baksheesh* for their seats on the roof.

Considering the view they had up here, two rupees was a small price to pay. While the Americans argued, the rich and varied treasures of the Keralan waterways were continually revealing themselves to the rest of us. Everywhere, lining the banks, were rows of jungle coco-palms, all swaying to and fro in the warm, gentle breeze. Their reflections appeared mirror-sharp in the calm, steel-blue waters, to be broken only by the passage of primitive canvas and wood craft, bearing Chinese cloth-sails.

In the shallower stretches, local men bathed by the bank, taking care to avoid the regular schools of giant jellyfish passing downstream. From narrow shaded canals, we passed into large, spacious inland lakes, and then towards green, verdant banks thronged with waving children from local Catholic missions, churches and schools. Stripped fishermen, standing waist-deep in the waters, stopped to greet us before casting out their wide, strong nets. Shoals of flying fish leapt and dove in the wake of the boat, their rhythmic action accompanied by the regular, hypnotic throb of the vessel's pumping engine. And all around us there were birds, all kinds of exotic birds, adding the final touch of sound and colour to this delightful scene.

Kevin's love of the water was really in evidence today. He was in raptures throughout the trip, and spent much of it thinking of possible designs for the boat he himself would build some day. One stretch of water was of particular fascination to him – where the water-lilies and algae had grown so dense that they covered the entire surface of the water like a bright green carpet. It seemed rather that our vessel had turned into a huge mechanical plough which was carving its way through a thick green swathe of meadow grassland.

The boat stopped just twice in the long eight-hour journey. At the first stop, Kevin tried to buy some food. All that he could come up with was a desiccated banana encased in a leathery pouch of dried batter. It looked obscene. And it tasted revolting. Kevin tried to donate it to a beggar, but the beggar took offence. Then he tried tossing it to a scrofulous dog foraging by the water-bank. But the dog took one sniff at it and ran away.

We reached Allepey at sunset, the last light filling the fields and pastures lining the waterway with an unearthly luminous-green glow. It was a fitting conclusion to a perfect day.

February 13th

Our second trip down the Keralan backwater – on from Allepey to Kottayam – was a good deal shorter than yesterday's but just as enjoyable. By way of variation, this stretch of water provided far more interesting views of native cargo boats. These were generally about fifty feet in length, shaped like canoes and round-bilged, and were propelled by small sprite-sails mounted well forward on punt-poles. The cargoes they carried, as best we could judge, were mostly bananas, cashew nuts, fish, logs, silt and various building materials like bricks, cement and solid blocks of cut stone.

Our lodgings tonight, the Kottayam Tourist Bungalow, were a hard slog to get to, but turned out to be well worth the effort. The large, spacious quarters we gained were, we learnt, originally used by British officers in the days of the Raj, and they still contained much antique Victorian and Edwardian furniture. They also contained, it must be added, armies of ants. But these didn't trouble us, so we left them well alone.

The hotel's resident cook told us he was a medical graduate unable to find any job outside of a kitchen. He served such an excellent meal, however, that Kevin ceased bemoaning the mosquito bites under his right kneecap and fell to with a will. Our meal finished, we both agree that we should shortly have to slow down the furious pace of our travels, and get some rest. So far, we had not stopped in any one place in India for more than three days.

February 14th

The 10.30am bus to Kumily failed to appear. Everybody expected it to appear, but it didn't. The information desk clerks shrugged at us, and said it had most certainly left in our direction. Why it never reached us was quite beyond them. And they seemed to have little idea of what was going on in the rest of the bus-station either. We had three long hours till the next bus in which to observe this confusing terminus, and we couldn't make head or tail of it.

Scores of different buses were arriving and departing all the time, and each one, as soon as it drew up, was surrounded by a melee of Indians trying to guess where it was going. None of the buses had any destinations posted, so the potential passengers were reduced to leaping up and down outside the driver's compartment shouting for information. By the time they had got it, and had realised that this was indeed their bus, it had already left. No one bus we observed stayed in the station for more than thirty seconds. Scores of hapless Indians trying to board these restless juggernauts were sent flying – briefcases,

baggage and all – back into the dust as with a crazed blast on
the air-horn and a screech of burning rubber, one bus after another tore out of the station.

Our long wait was made even more tedious by the arrival of
a loquacious old Indian who gave us his entire life history,
plentifully sprinkled with sentimental reminiscences of his
service with the Gurkhas in the good old days of the Raj. But
our relief in escaping from him onto the bus – when it at last
put in an appearance – was short-lived. A vast tidal wave of
humanity swept aboard along with us. The next four and a half
hours, spent squashed like sardines in the rear seats, were absolute torture.

After a lifetime of soft, easy living in the West, one's buttocks take an awful hammering out here. Backpacking around
India is just one long round of sitting on bone-hard, chafing,
bruising and generally uncomfortable seats – whether in buses,
or trains, or restaurants or cinemas. There is no such thing as a
padded seat in the whole country. And if this isn't bad enough,
an enforced crash-diet as one travels through Tamil Nadu and
Kerala strips away the last protective layers of fat from around
your rump, so that a roller-coaster ride on a bumpy bus like
this one is enough to reduce your bum to a bruised jelly of destroyed tissue. No wonder fat people are so envied in India.
They must be the only people able to sit down or travel in
comfort.

Kumily lies at the summit of a high mountain plateau, and
is approached via beautiful green tea-plantations, stretching
out for miles in all directions. With the approach of dusk, their
earlier lawn-green hue gives way slowly to a deep shade of
pine. It was while leaning out of my window to observe this
that the five Indians sharing my back seat toppled over asleep
on my shoulders like a row of dominoes. I spent the remainder

of the journey helplessly pinned against the window.

At Kumily, we booked into the Lake Queen Tourist Home. It had a 'luxury' restaurant downstairs, but when we went down for super it was completely empty. We split up to send search parties out for the waiter, but we couldn't find him. Giving up, we went out into the street looking for another restaurant. But then the whole town suddenly went black. A nearby magnetic storm had caused a total power-cut. Stumbling back into our dark room, we could hear it buzzing with mosquitoes. Kumily, remarked Kevin prophetically, was going to give us problems.

We went to bed. It was still pitch-black outside. Within our room, the overhead fan whirred round with a quiet, insistent hum. Otherwise, all was silent. I closed my eyes. Long minutes passed. Then Kevin's voice shattered the peace. 'I can hear a mosquito,' he announced. The lights came back on. 'I got undressed for bed,' continued Kevin, 'but now I've heard that mosquito, I'm getting dressed again.'

Before the lights were extinguished again, I took one last look at Kevin. He was not taking any chances with those mosquitoes. Not only had he turned the air-fan on full blast, which pinned us both securely to our beds, but his body was now swathed in three layers of clothing and smeared with a thick yellow paste of 'Odomos'. Surrounded by a glowing circle of smouldering smoke-coils, his bed had taken on the aspect of a funeral pyre. And on top of it lay Kevin, his arms peacefully folded over his jaundiced, overdressed body, looking like a deceased Eskimo.

February 15th

Today we hired bicycles and rode out to Thekkidy game reserve, hoping to see the wild animals which graze on the banks
of the Periyar Lake. I was just beginning to enjoy this excursion, cycling quietly through the calm, peaceful woodland
roads, when a convoy of screeching Forestry Commission
jeeps and trucks roared past, sending all the monkeys and birds
resting in the treetops flying for cover. Their behaviour bewil-
dered us. For it was the Forestry Commission who had posted
signs all along this road instructing tourists like us to '*Keep
quiet* in the forest in order to see and enjoy the animals at their
best.'

On the way to the lake, we stopped at Periyar's 25th anniversary 'Jubilee Exhibition.' This comprised a clay elephant
lurking in the undergrowth, a gold model tiger with a jolly be-
tel-red grin, a giant wicker peacock and a plaster giraffe with
tree branches sprouting from its head like a set of weird ant-
lers. The 'exhibition' hut itself contained just a few photos of
animal species wiped out when the lake's dam was built, and
three glass cages containing respectively a stuffed tiger, a
stuffed bear and a limp ex-cobra!

The information office at the Forestry Commission in
Thekkidy refused to give us any information at all. It *had* the
information all right. It just wasn't handing it out. The official
at the desk told me they only had 'limited stocks'. I spent a
half-hour trying to persuade him to part with some of his limited stock, and was rewarded with a single information leaflet.
I felt quite pleased with myself: no other tourist in the area had
managed to get one.

The Periyar Lake is an artificial lake built by the British
about 90 years ago. You can see it is an artificial lake because

scores of jagged tree stumps and branches still point their spectral fingers above its surface. Before its construction, these trees must have been a formidable size, for even in this pre-monsoon season the depth of the lake was some eighty feet.

We booked tickets on the 4pm boat round the lake, which promised best views of the wild elephants, water buffalo and even tigers who tend to come to water at this time of day. We were, however, to be disappointed. The frantic Indian contingent of tourists aboard our vessel maintained such a loud volume of shrill, penetrating conversation that every animal on its way down to the lake did an immediate about-turn. We saw a flock of retreating wild pigs, a couple of retreating baboons, and a distant retreating elephant. Even the flying fish which came near the boat rapidly flew off in the opposite direction.

The boat's gentle captain soon became tired of his noisy passengers also, and engaged me in conversation, probably to steady his nerves. He was a sensitive man whose broad features and high forehead denoted a warm nature and keen intelligence. He told me that he was fully qualified to be a captain of a ship on the open sea, but lack of jobs compelled him to work on this small sightseeing boat for just £50 per month. He only got to see his family, who lived back down the waterways at Kottayam, once in each month. Despite this, he managed to hold a cheerful, lively conversation and I reflected on how pleasant it was to talk feely to an Indian man about his life, his hopes and his dreams without the usual barriers that tended to go up between the average Indian and the average Western tourist.

Back on land, we returned to the information centre to book its advertised 'elephant ride' for tomorrow morning. But we hit another brick wall. The information officer, irritated at being woken from his afternoon nap in the side office, came out to tell us there *was* no elephant ride. 'Why not?' we enquired. He yawned at us and replied: 'So sorry – elephant *sick*!' Well, we should have guessed. Kevin sent the elephant his best wishes for a speedy recovery, and we cycled back to Kumily.

February 16th

We returned to the site of Periyar Lake again this morning, ready to start our 'forest trek' at nine o' clock. We were both eagerly looking forward to this: at last, we would now get to see the wild animals in the nature reserve up close. Or would we?

There were nine of us in the small trekking party, led by a tiny Indian guide wearing the most enormous pair of ex-Army issue shorts. He took us over a series of low hills skirting the lake, and then plunged us into a thick burnt-green jungle with strict instructions not to disturb the wildlife. But he needn't have worried. We didn't see any wildlife to disturb. For three and a half gruelling hours we trudged through the damp arboreal vegetation with not even a sniff of a wild animal. Sorry, we did see a solitary distant pig and a pair of tree-monkeys too lazy or indifferent to scurry away at our approach. And we did see some elephant droppings. We saw an awful lot of elephant droppings. The whole trek path was plastered with elephant droppings.

Every so often, the diminutive guide would gather us around him in a discreet huddle and hiss: 'Look! Tiger footprint! There is a tiger nearby!' Much more commonly, however, he would whisper: 'Look! Elephant dropping! There are elephant nearby!'

Kevin and I decided to make our own amusement from

now on. We went into the 'Disco' barbers in Kumily high street, and had all our hair shaved off. The sight of two crazy Westerners going bald created quite a stir in the local community. A swaying crowd of curious Indians gathered in the street outside to watch.

'If your mother could only see you now!' I remarked as Kevin's gleaming, tonsured scalp came into view.

'Actually,' came his bald comment, 'I did have my hair cut close once, and my father wouldn't speak to me for three days!'

I considered this, and suggested he send a photograph of his bald head home right now.

'If you send it off now,' I helpfully suggested, 'your father will have six whole weeks to cool off before you get back to England!'

I was doubled up with laughter the whole time Kevin was in the barber's chair. When the flashing scalpel came my way, however, it was quite a different story. I opened my mouth to protest, but it was too late. The first ridge of shiny bare scalp had already appeared in the barber's mirror.

The crowd outside got very excited when we returned to their midst, our domes gleaming like two new pins The whole street reverberated with joyful cries of 'Kung Fu!' and 'Shaolin!' and upwards of a hundred people followed us down the dark road. I became concerned. And I became even more concerned when I saw Saint Anthony coming the other way. He was lit up with coloured bulbs and strapped to the front of a jeep. The jeep was escorted by a mass of candle-bearing schoolchildren singing militant carols. Firecrackers were going off all over the place, and the jeep was led up the road by a band of determined-looking musicians. This lot wasn't going to move aside for anything. A head-on collision between

Catholic and Buddhist acolytes appeared imminent.

Suddenly, a miraculous event occurred to avert disaster. Just as the two crowds were about to clash, a pair of itinerant donkeys appeared between them and began copulating in the middle of the high street. 'Golly!' exclaimed Kevin. 'I've got to get a photograph of *that!*' And as he bolted ahead to snap the performing donkeys, both crowds shuddered violently to a halt, mere yards from achieving impact with each other. Kevin (and the mules) had narrowly averted a full-scale riot. They had done it by arousing the curiosity of every Indian in the vicinity. Everybody was staring at Kevin amazed. They were, I guessed, all thinking the same thing: 'Try getting *that* one developed in our country, Englishman!' ...But he did.

February 17th

We came into Cochin this morning. Our bus there was full of Indians staring at Kevin's bald head (I wisely kept my cap on). Arriving, we moved into the Hotel Elite. Our room was stark and simple, but downstairs was the best western-style restaurant in town. It even provided Kevin with a cheese sandwich. The cheese came out of a fridge, and was hygienically wrapped in foil. Kevin went into a transport of delight, and I didn't hear any more about cheese sandwiches for the next week. The service at the Elite's restaurant was excellent too. It is famous among foreign travellers as the only restaurant in India where the waiter always smiles at you and always remembers your order.

A couple of Indian chaps joined us at our table. At first, we thought they had come just to stare at our bald heads – like everyone else we had met today – but they only wanted to be friendly. We ended up having a long, enjoyable conversation about commerce, politics and economics. Unfortunately, just as it was getting really interesting, an Australian called Dave turned up to queer the pitch. He asked our Indian friends if it was true what he had heard, that seventy per cent of all Indian men were gay, because caste restrictions preventing contact with Indian women made it impossible for them to be anything else. The two Indians looked at each other in dismay, and silently got up and left the table. Dave asked us if he had said anything wrong. It was our turn to look at each other in dismay and leave the table.

It was this evening, over supper at the Hotel Seagull, that Kevin's recent cheerfulness finally evaporated. Things started well enough: he gave his order for fish and chips to the waiter, and began the usual procedure of picking up spelling errors in the menu. This was a good one too – SCRABBLED EGGS, SCHERADE BEEF (shredded beef), BUFFALEW FRY, and LEMON SOD (lemon soda) – but then the waiter came back again. He had forgotten Kevin's order. So he took it a second time, but then reappeared a while later to say that he had forgotten it again. These consistent attacks of amnesia however were as nothing to his major transgression: not serving Kevin enough chips, and giving him a small black object which was supposed to be a fish fillet.

'What's *this?*' said Kevin, snarling dangerously at the waiter.

'It is fish and chips,' answered the waiter.

Kevin swept up the plate and marched it into the kitchen. 'I want the complaint book!' he told the harassed-looking manger.

'So sorry,' replied the manager. 'There is no complaint book.'

Kevin thrust the plate at him. 'Then I want more chips,' he demanded. 'And you can replace this morsel of fish with a bigger bit. A bit which isn't burnt black like this one!'

The manager demurred politely, saying, 'Fish not burnt.'

This got Kevin going. 'Oh yes, it is!' he raged, sweeping the offending cinder off the plate and waving it under the manager's bushy moustache for added emphasis. '*This is a burnt fillet!*'

'No, no!' protested the manager, recovering the fillet out of Kevin's hand. 'It is burnt on the *batter,* yes, but the fish inside, it is not burnt!'

He passed the fillet back to Kevin, who stamped his foot and howled: 'IT'S BLOODY BURNT!' before flinging it to a nearby waiter. The charred ember of fish was now rapidly going the rounds, being passed, thrown, fingered, dissected, picked at and returned by five different people, including the cook, the cook's assistant and a trainee waiter.

Kevin waited until the fish returned into his possession, and then brandished it dramatically in the air. 'Would *you* pay 11 rupees for this rubbish?' he cried. 'Just look at it – it wouldn't feed a *canary!*' The distraught manager waggled his head furiously in answer, though whether to agree with or dispute Kevin's allegations it was impossible to say. As he stretched out his hands to make his case, Kevin decisively deposited the burnt fillet in them and stormed off into the night.

February 19th

Today we hired bicycles, and rode through Cochin's narrow backstreets to Mattancherry. The city's oldest synagogue here was a simple white-painted structure notable for its beautiful interior of suspended oil-lamps, hand-painted floor tiling and superb brass-work. It was now little more than a museum piece, however, the original strong Jewish community in Cochin having shrunk (at the time of writing) to just thirty-three members.

By contrast, Mattancherry's 'Dutch Palace' (not Dutch at all, but Portuguese) is full of remarkable 16th century wall-murals, one of which shows the god Shiva on lascivious top form, all eight of his hands busily at work on the private parts of eight receptive handmaidens.

Returning, Kevin and I hurried to Cochin station to catch the 7.30pm train to Mettapulayam. But we needn't have rushed. The first people we spoke to on the platform informed us: 'Train postponed – now arriving at 8.45.' We thought we had better check this, so asked another group of people. They assured us: 'No, postponement now *cancelled* – train, it is leaving at 7.30 as scheduled!' Finally, we came to the platform waiting-room, where a chorus of fifteen rail employees told us: 'Train is most certainly *postponed* – will now arrive at 8.30!'

Well, they should have known. The train did arrive at 8.30, much to the surprise of all the other passengers expecting it an hour earlier or fifteen minutes later. And the ten-hour journey to Mettapulayam, via Coimbatore, passed very smoothly in-deed. It was so smooth in fact, that we both managed to sleep right through it.

February 20th

Passing up into the mountains on the famous 'toy train' from Mettapulayam to the hill-station of Ooty was an unforgettable experience. The railway runs a special 'rack and pinion' track up the mountain ascent, a third 'chain' rail passing in between the usual pair of narrow gauge rails. The engine is placed behind the carriages, and pushes them up the steep track, using the grip of the extra rail to maintain constant traction all the way up to the town of Ooty, two thousand feet above.

From the open windows of the miniature blue-and-white wooden carriages, we looked down over a series of magnificent mountain, valley, woodland and village views. The five and a half hour journey passed with surprising speed. Partly because we were deeply in conversation with a young Indian sharing our carriage. Well-spoken, athletic and intelligent, he told us he was just visiting his home country at present, being currently employed in Australia.

'I am well-qualified,' he said, 'but I cannot obtain well-paid work here. Also, I might waste ten years working in some low-paid job in India, only to be passed over for promotion when my superior dies by someone of a higher caste who has no experience of the job whatsoever. There is simply no incentive for the well-qualified man in this country.'

He moved on to explain the Indian caste system, and to tell us how socially and emotionally restrictive it was for men and women alike. Indian men, he maintained, often only had their first real contact with women when they got married, and this generally didn't happen until their late 20s or early 30s. As for the women, the caste system forced them into difficult dependency on their husbands. 'If you gave this country some social security and created more jobs for women,' he stated, 'then many wives here would tell their husbands to get lost, and would walk out. Because of the present inequality, very few Indian marriages I have seen are truly happy, and many of them are downright miserable!'

Arriving in Ooty Town, we booked into the popular

YMCA, strolled round the nearby Botanical Gardens and saw a twenty thousand year old fossilised tree trunk (it looked like a gift-wrapped plank), then retired to bed for a long rest.

February 21st

Today had an inauspicious beginning. Much in need of a shower, I had ordered hot water for 7 this morning. But the room-boy had forgotten. I had to follow him all round the hostel in the freezing cold, dressed only in a towel, just to get the opportunity to jog his memory. Later, now armed with my bucket of hot water, I stood in the icy shower-room and enjoyed a good wash. I was watched throughout by a pair of tiny frogs, both frozen solid to the walls.

Ooty, like other Indian hill-stations, is a favourite holiday resort. People flock here in the summer to go boating on the lake, to ride horses, to play golf or simply to admire the beautiful scenery. We decided to start with the lake.

Just as we reached the boating quay, we suddenly ran into Charlie, our little brown waiter from the Village Restaurant in Mahabilapuram. He embraced us with the enthusiasm of a biblical shepherd recovering some long-lost sheep. Which was an appropriate analogy, since he was presently working by the lake at a shop selling 'Christ Eucalyptus Oil'. After introducing us proudly to all his friends, he sent us on to a cha-shop for some teas with a promise to return shortly. Kevin gaped astonished at the stunted little cha-wallah, who was carefully washing an old one-rupee note in a basin, and then hanging it over a hot tea-pot spout to dry out.

Ooty lake is full of ponies. Everywhere you go round here, there is a pony breathing down your neck. I was just complaining about ponies over my cup of coffee when, perfectly on cue, an Indian appeared leading a pony. 'You want pony ride?' he offered. 'Pony ride?' I echoed. 'Ah!' confirmed the Indian. 'No,' said I, and he said 'No?' I said 'No,' and he said 'No?' again. I tried to bring the conversation to a close, stating firmly: 'No. No ponies!' but he just said 'Huh?' and dragged his pony even closer. 'Look, this is getting us nowhere!' I ranted at him, 'just take your pony somewhere else. It's just blown its nose in my coffee!'

Charlie came to the rescue. He got rid of the pony-man, arranged to meet us later, and saw us onto a boat for the lake. Sculling out from the shore, we were followed for some distance by friendly Indians in other boats hollering 'What is your name?' and 'Where are you coming from?' but we soon rowed beyond them, and found a quiet spot on the far side of the wide lake, where we were not disturbed. For a very enjoyable hour, we sat back and relaxed while the cool breeze played on the calm, clear water and the warm sun played on the backs of our bald, polished skulls. Kevin said that this part of the lake reminded him of the Norfolk Broads.

Back on land again, we went to the Liberty Cinema to see an entertaining film called *Shaolin Temple*. It was all about armed Buddhist monks reluctantly slaughtering half the local militia in order to save their temple. At the first break in the film, the lights came on, our caps came off to give our bald heads an airing, and the serried ranks of grinning Indians behind us gave a concerted shout of 'Shaolin!' – thinking we were Buddhist monks. Then they left the cinema, thinking that the break was an interval. But it wasn't the interval at all, just the second reel being loaded. Everybody quickly piled back in the cinema again. And then, when the real interval came, nobody trusted it and everybody stayed rooted to their seats. Finally, when the film came to an end, they all got up again and made to leave the cinema, only to discover it wasn't the end of the picture at all, so they had to wade back inside and sit down again until it had really finished.

Having returned to the YMCA for supper, we met a young English couple called Tim and Jill. They had also recently returned from Thekkidy Wildlife Reserve. Whilst there, they had decided to avoid the recommended guided forest trek (the one where all you see is wildlife droppings) and instead opted to go exploring on their own. They were just wondering where all the animals were, when Jill had to stop and lean on a tree to get a splinter out of her foot. Only it wasn't a tree she was leaning on, but a baby elephant. And its mother was standing right next to it, looking not all pleased. Tim and Jill fled hot-foot back to their lodge. This was the luxurious Forest Lake Hotel, and here they recovered from their shock – casually observing elephants safely watering on the other side of a deep ditch – along with all the other guests in the hotel. Then they noticed that two bull elephants had materialised on *their* side of the ditch. And both of them suddenly gave a crazed bellow and thundered towards the terrorised guests. Everyone scrambled back up to their huts, where they hid quaking while the maddened elephants tore up the lodge's garden shrubbery, battered down a couple of trees, and made repeated thundering assaults on the building itself. Tiring of this, the massive beasts had contented themselves with patrolling round the lodge for the rest of the night – peering in windows and snuffling through doors – while Tim and Jill (and every other guest) lay shivering in fear beneath their bedclothes.

February 22ⁿᵈ

The V.K. Bakery in Ooty's Commercial Road serves just about the best cakes and patisseries in India. As we arrived this morning, a batch of fresh mutton puff-pastry rolls had just emerged from the ovens. We rapidly disposed of these, then moved on to a piping-hot loaf each, followed by some appetising chocolate cake. We ate continuously for two hours. I had never seen Kevin looking so happy.

To work off this excess of food, we bussed up to the nearby Dodabetta Height, took in the marvellous views of Ooty Town and surroundings from the summit, and then commenced a long two-hour stroll down by foot. This was a delightful walk, the cool breeze sending shimmers of sparkling light through the coppery-gold forest glades and rustling gently through the brilliant green foliage of roadside pine and evergreens. Further down, the road opened up into a dry, dusty clearing, with gangs of local workers chipping away busily at the side of the mountain, building safer highways. On the stepped farmland below them, other families of workers were tilling the soil and planting crops. As we passed, they all looked up to give us a smiling wave of welcome.

The only blot on this calm scene was the regular succession of noisy tourist coaches blaring up the mountain passes. Air-horns on at full blast, and egged on by their loads of cheering Indian tourists, these insensitive juggernauts tore up the hill like there was no tomorrow. Kevin became so piqued with them that he lay in wait and gave one of them a sudden shrill blast on the plastic green police-whistle he'd bought earlier in the bazaar. The victim driver was so stunned by this unexpected rearguard action that he almost plunged his busload of singing Indians right off the edge of the cliff.

We returned to the V.K. Bakery to meet Charlie. He came bouncing down the road just as we were seeing off another helping of chocolate cake. We took him to a nearby Chinese restaurant, and treated him to a feast of scrambled egg on toast.

Charlie was an eighteen-year-old Brahmin youth, whose neat and smart appearance, coupled with his academic, inquiring mind, testified to his high-caste status. Not only was he a talented amateur artist, but he also had an encyclopaedic knowledge of Indian history and mythology. Having heard in Mahabilapuram that I was an eminent English professor (someone's idea of a joke), he felt bound to share the entire fruits of his knowledge with me. It was indeed fortunate that I was interested to hear about Hindu gods and goddesses, because Charlie was of a very determined disposition. He was going to tell me all about them, whether I cared to hear or not.

I was particularly taken with the parable he quoted from one of India's foremost poets. This parable, Charlie told us, explained the fundamental reason for India's continuing poverty.

'In this poem there is a frog,' he recounted, 'and the frog lives and dies in a beautiful lotus blossom – never seeing, never knowing, that there is rich honey in it. He lives instead by eating mud and insects. And he dies never knowing of the rich bed of honey he has been sitting on his whole life.'

'This parable,' Charlie went on to explain, 'is meaning that we people in India do not understand or see the good things around us, or the wealth of our heritage and culture. Instead, we are always looking and searching for bad things only. Thus, India is eating the same meal of bad things for thousands of years. She is still squatting in the mud and dirt of her ignorance. And, worst of all, because her people are not seeing the wealth of their own knowledge and culture, they are still allowing foreigners to steal the fruit of it!'

We eventually steered Charlie off the subject of philosophy, and got him talking about his plans for the future. He told us he was presently doing correspondence course studies, in preparation for a 'restaurant' he was going to establish by Ooty Lake. We asked him how he expected to set up a restaurant on wages of just Rs500 (about £40) a month. He bent forward and told us in a surreptitious whisper how he was making Rs400 'extra' a month by overcharging people for Christ Eucalyptus Oil.

Charlie's single-minded preoccupation with his restaurant plan rendered him quite deaf to any suggestions we might have concerning it. Kevin tried to advise him on the best way to cook fast-food chips, but Charlie wasn't listening. He was quite impervious to any new ideas. He was going to do it his way. The only thing that worried me about his plans was his constant talk of the 'cart' he would be bringing up from the plains for his new restaurant. Kevin and I spent much of the evening trying to work out what this 'cart' involved. We eventually discovered that it wasn't a cart at all, but a mobile van. Charlie was planning to set up India's very first five-star mobile snack bar. And with his kind of total dedication, who was going to stop him?

February 23rd

Today we moved northward to the 'incense' city of Mysore. Here, we found lodgings at the popular Durbar Lodge. Charging just twenty rupees (£1.50) each, this place was a real find. Not only did our room have a balcony giving a fine view of the streets and bazaars below, but the lodge had *two* attached restaurants. Visiting the downstairs one, we came across another deliciously mis-spelt menu – offering SLICED CHI (chips) WITH VEGTABEWES, CHINEES CHOPSY CHICKEN, and (our favourite) EGG-N-BRAIN. The beverages on offer were equally strange: they included BORN VITA and PAIN APPLE JUICE.

The other restaurant was on the roof. We had our evening meal here, listening to tinny western music playing in the background. We were just looking down and commenting on how bright and busy the street-life below was, when we caught sight of the beggar woman. She was lying in the middle of the road, inviting death under the wheels of all the traffic roaring past, and she held a small baby in her arms. If this was not disturbing enough, local people were dodging speeding buses and lorries to drop a few coins into her outstretched hand, and then simply wandering off again.

It was the child which finally moved Kevin to action. From the start, we had both agreed never to intervene in the customs or disputes of this country, not only because we may well be misinterpreting the situation but also because we had heard of Indians turning violent when foreigners attempted to interfere in their private business. But with the life of a helpless child at stake, all such considerations were abandoned.

'I've got to do something about this!' declared Kevin. And, rising suddenly from his seat, he stormed off down into the street.

Following on, I found him a minute later standing in the middle of a large crowd. He was soundly berating the beggar woman for exposing her baby to certain death in the traffic. But she just smiled back sweetly at him, and remained laid out in the middle of the road. Fortunately, just as the crowd were starting to turn nasty against Kevin, a local Indian doctor chanced along. He calmly lifted the child off the dusty tarmac and deposited it safely on a nearby kerb. Satisfied, Kevin returned back to the restaurant.

February 25th

Early this afternoon, we caught the train from Mysore up to Londa. The journey, at least in the early stages, was very pleasant. We were sharing a compartment with a young Indian commerce student, his sister, and her two-year-old child. The sister was nicknamed 'Mogadon' by Kevin because the train journey lasted twenty-six hours, and she managed to sleep through twenty-four of them. Also in our compartment was a young Portuguese couple who wanted us to visit Francis Xavier's remains (or rather, what *remains* of his remains, since many of his bones have been swiped by 'holy relic' hunters!) in Old Goa.

As we headed north, mile upon mile of rich, arable farmland came into view from the train window. Hours passed with us seeing a bare handful of Indian people working the land. In this deserted hinterland, at least, there was evidently no risk of overpopulation for some considerable time.

At 6.30pm we stopped at Mandargere. And stayed stopped. A train ahead had been derailed, and we were told to expect a long delay. The delay was to last nine hours, but I had no foreknowledge of that and began conversing with a couple of curious schoolchildren staring in my window. What a terrible mistake! Before I knew what had happened, my audience had increased to twenty-eight people. They had all collected to ask me what my name was, and would I play them some disco music on my Walkman. For a time, all this attention was marvellous stuff for the ego, but I soon came to feel like a zoo exhibit. Being stared at from behind the bars of the compartment window for hours on end made me feel like some rare caged animal newly brought to captivity. My persistent fan club simply wouldn't go away. I went to look at my reflection in the train toilet's cracked mirror, sure that somehow I had acquired Kevin's likeness to Sean Connery. But no, I hadn't. I was at a complete loss to explain my sudden unwelcome popularity.

I returned to the compartment and found that my vast audience, far from going away, had actually increased. Now there were thirty-two grinning faces staring in at me. I pulled the window blind down to indicate that the show was over. But when I pulled it up again ten minutes later, they were still all there, patiently waiting for the curtain to rise on another performance. Kevin smirked that he could have made a fortune selling tickets outside on the platform. But he wasn't smirking for long. He soon had problems of his own.

Kevin's problems came in one small package – a loud, precocious seven-year-old boy who had just finished driving his father to distraction in the adjoining compartment, and who now came over to inflict the same fate on the hapless Kevin. We nicknamed him 'Mowgli' – he had just the right kind of irksome, wide-eyed, jug-eared, clean-cut and generally over-curious enthusiasm that immediately endears itself to hungry jungle animals and immediately sends adult human beings flying for cover.

Mowgli took an instant shine to Kevin. He started off on a pleasantly low key, bringing over all his pictures of racing cars, his calendar with racing cars all over it, and his toy racing car for Kevin to admire. But then, without any warning at all, he swung into top gear and accused Kevin of being a wealthy Iranian.

'You are Iranian!' declared the obnoxious youngster. 'And you have lots of money!'

Kevin gaped at him open-mouthed. 'I am *not* Iranian!' he replied hotly. 'And I am *not* rich! I live in England and I own just one bicycle and two Beatles records. These are my only possessions.'

'No! No! You are rich!' shouted Mowgli, jumping up and down on his seat in his thrill of the hunt. 'You are rich, and you are Iranian man *pretending* to be coming from England! I know!'

It was now 9pm, and I took a peek through the window blind, but my fan club was still there, silently waiting. What with this, and the arrival of Mowgli, I wondered what else could happen? No sooner had I made room for this idle speculation, then something else did. An unwholesome individual with a greasy smile slid into our compartment, and sat down next to me. Grinning all the while, he began playfully fingering the combination lock on my rucksack and expertly ran his hands over my belongings to assess their possible worth. I was just beginning to lose my cool when he came to the end of his inventory, flashed me a last brilliant smile, complimented me on having such a strong lock on my bags, and went off in search of some easier prey.

By this point, my nerves were beginning to crack. I felt surrounded. I didn't even dare go out onto the platform to buy a banana, for fear of being mobbed by the crowd of devoted acolytes outside. I sent Kevin to make the purchase instead, and immediately regretted it. Now I was stuck with Mowgli.

'Where is your friend?' enquired the awesomely tedious brat, referring to Kevin.

'I don't know,' I replied thinly.

'Where is your friend?' came the same demand.

I replied that I didn't know, and so he asked me again. He seemed to think I was stowing Kevin away in hiding somewhere. For what reason, I couldn't guess. What was so special about Kevin anyway? He didn't really like racing cars, and if there was anyone who looked less like a rich Iranian than Kevin, I had yet to meet him.

When Kevin reappeared, the frustrated youngster gave a shrill yelp of joy and pounced on him, sending my banana flying out of the window and into the hands of the waiting throng outside. They were so pleased at this unexpected token of my esteem that they rattled and knocked away on the blinded window for a further hour or two, in hope of more bananas, before finally going off to their beds.

Before I at last drifted off to sleep myself, I listened to Kevin giving a lecture on economics to the eternally curious Mowgli. The little monster's gurgles of delight as he absorbed this fresh store of knowledge sent my fragile nerves to the brink of total collapse. Mowgli seemed to *know* everything there was to know about everything. He did, however, have one vital gap in his encyclopaedic knowledge which he was determined to plug. He wanted to know the price of trousers in Iran.

'How much cost your trousers in Iran?' pressed the gruesome brat.

Poor Kevin, by now worn down to a frazzle, eyed him wearily. He had long since given up denying he came from Iran (it simply wasn't worth the trouble), but he felt he must make one last plea to the child's better nature.

'What does it matter how much trousers cost in Iran?' he pleaded. 'And why do you always want to know how much everything *costs?* After all, there's a lot more to life than *money!'*

Mowgli thought deeply for a moment, and then brightly enquired 'What?'

Kevin groaned in despair, and rolled over to sleep.

February 26th

Kevin was still asleep when the insufferable Mowgli skipped back into our compartment this morning. He didn't stay asleep much longer. Mowgli bent close to his ear and bellowed down it: 'Wake UP! Wake UP! Train is not working! Train is not working because there is *no engine attached!*'

I complimented Mowgli on his brilliant powers of deduction – the train had been stuck at Arsikere with no engine attached for the past two hours. Kevin, having started suddenly awake at Mowgli's announcement and having banged his head on the top of his bunk, was not pleased at all. He met the child's repeated requests for a letter from Iran with a low growl of displeasure. Only momentarily shaken, the incredible infant bounced back to plan our whole route home to England for us, using a beaten-up old atlas with racing cars all over it. It was only when we came to Hubli some hours later that Kevin managed to tear himself away, leaning out of the carriage window to load up a hatful of roasted peanuts handed over by the platform vendor. But even this caused problems.

'Have you change for ten rupees?' enquired Kevin of the vendor.

'No change,' came the brief reply.

'No change! He has no change!' echoed Mowgli dutifully, clapping his little hands in excitement. Kevin's peanuts began quivering in his grasp, as he fought down his compulsion to do murder.

It was shortly after Mogadon made her single, fleeting excursion into the world of wakefulness that her young baby's green underpants dropped unexpectedly on Kevin's head from the bunk above, reminding him that he was due a trip to the mirror. 'Lend me your comb, will you?' he said. I stared at him, disbelieving. '*What* hair?' I enquired. 'The hair on my head!' he replied. '*What* hair on your head? I persisted. 'You haven't *got* any hair on your head! You're *bald*, man! You're just like me – as bald as the proverbial coot!' But he wouldn't believe me. He would have the comb, and go off to the mirror to see for himself. And when he returned (still bald), all he had to say for himself was: 'I told you! I've got a really nice head of hair now! Yes, not at all bad for nine days...'

I disembarked at Hubli, and went off down the platform in search of food. Both of us were by now very much the worse for wear, and had not – apart from peanuts and bananas – eaten for a whole day. To my great relief, I came across an Indian on the platform cooking delicious fresh omelettes (in fruit-bread sandwiches!) on a gas stove. I waited patiently for a couple of these, and then turned to re-board the rain. But it wasn't there. It appeared to have left without me. I stood there like a lemon, holding two dripping omelettes in one hand and two dripping ice-creams in the other, wondering how on earth I was going to get to Londa now, with just five rupees and no ticket in my pocket.

Minutes later, the train returned. It had just gone away for a short while to dump some excess carriages. Curiously, I hadn't been too bothered when it had vanished. After twenty-five claustrophobic hours on the train, it was something of a relief to be off it for a while, even in such worrying circumstances. Back on the train, Kevin surveyed the melted ice-cream with a marked lack of enthusiasm. His eyes were glazing over with the exhaustion of this marathon journey. I could see he had had enough of it also. Things must be bad if Kevin goes off his food.

The train finally reached Londa at 5.30pm, two hours earlier than anticipated. This enabled us to catch the very last bus into Margao tonight. And it was a surprisingly pleasant trip. The advantages of travelling on Indian buses at night are numerous – it is cool, there are always lots of seats, it is much quieter than usual, and one is allowed to smoke.

We booked into the Tourist Hostel in Margao at 10.30pm, just in time to get a beer and some food at the attached restaurant. After three hours on the night bus, we were again very hungry and very thirsty. The beer went straight to Kevin's head, and he went to sleep the moment his head hit the pillow.

I was just preparing to go to sleep myself when I noticed the cockroach. It was a very big cockroach, quite the largest I had yet seen, and it was waving its antennae at me from the top of a chest of drawers. I was quite surprised to see it, because the rest of the room – including the normal source of cockroaches, the toilet – was immaculately clean. I was even more surprised when it moved from the chest of drawers, and scuttled up Kevin's bed to take up position on his big toe. But what surprised me most of all was when it did a sudden dash right up the length of Kevin's body, ending with a rapid circuit round his bald head. It came to rest on his right ear.

I felt moved to comment. 'Kevin! Kevin! Wake up!' I shouted. 'There's a three-inch cockroach sitting on your right ear!'

Kevin moaned, and opened one eye. 'So what?' he mumbled. And went straight back to sleep.

February 27th

We left Margao at 10am, boarding a bus on to Colva Beach – Goa's most famous coastal resort. The bus was crowded with wiry Portuguese housewives carrying home large baskets of fish, rice, sugar, melons and other provisions, recently purchased from Margao's bustling street markets.

At Colva, we took a simple room at Sabfran Cottages, recommended to us by Tim and Jill. Apart from the rats darting in and out during their time there, they reckoned this an ideal place to stay at in Goa. We were welcomed by a stout, energetic, sunny-faced individual who turned out to be Mr Sabfran himself. We asked him where he kept his rats, and was there a pig farm under the toilet? He said he didn't have any rats, and was fond of pigs, so didn't keep these either. After all the disconcerting stories we had heard about Goan pigs, this news came as a blessed relief. We moved our bags in right away.

In the cottage room next door lived a pale, thin and hesitant Frenchman called Francois. He had a good excuse for looking so pallid. He had just recovered from a severe bout of typhoid, contracted from drinking contaminated soda water on the beach. He had come to live with Mr Sabfran because there was a resident doctor next door. The doctor' fees, however, were rapidly reducing Francois to penury. He had already gone through Rs2800 ((£200) and would shortly have so little left that he would have to return to France.

Down the road, we once more bumped into our friend Andrew. This was the fifth, and final, time that our paths crossed. India has such a strange tendency for reuniting people time and again in the course of their travels. They all seem to be going in the same direction, like a flock of migratory birds. It was therefore little surprise to find Andrew in Goa. We had almost been expecting him.

Andrew told us he was having problems with his accommodation here. The lodge he was staying at made him nervous. Its real name was The Tourist Nest, but the locals had nicknamed it 'Death Cottage'. Alarmed, he wanted to know why. When he found out, he immediately started looking out new digs.

Apparently, this lodge had been run by a young Portuguese couple up until last Christmas. At this time, the jealous husband, suspecting an illicit liaison between his young wife and one of the new waiters, had stuck a carving knife in the waiter's chest. (The 'murder room' in which this occurred, by the way, was offered to Andrew on his arrival.) The poor waiter had crawled out of the lodge and bled to death on the garden veranda. News of his grisly demise spread fast. The local people, many of whom were friends or relatives, took an extremely dim view of his premature passage from this world. They began making midnight forays into the lodge's grounds, cutting down palm trees in the front garden, painting its walls with "get out of town!" warnings to the landlord, and eventually (thought this was never quite proven) murdering his mother, who was discovered suffocated in her bed one morning. The distraught young wife, who had started most of the trouble, adopted a twenty-four year old Indian boy with delusions of grandeur (he thought he was Clint Eastwood) to compensate herself for all this tragedy. But he too was found dead one morning, in equally mysterious circumstances. The husband, meanwhile, had gone to jail for murdering the waiter. Shortly after the expiry of 'Clint', he too died. Somebody had managed to murder him in his cell. The local constabulary finally decided that 'foul play' was being perpetrated here, but they were far too late to do anything about it. The whole family, apart from the young wife, was dead.

Later, we went down to Colva Beach. This is one of the longest beaches in India – just one continuous stretch of golden sand for an incredible distance of eighteen kilometres. Entering the sea here is like getting into a nice warm bath. The fierce pounding waves common in other parts of India's coastline, say at Madras or Mahabilapuram, are little in evidence here. Colva Beach is the nearest thing to paradise that India can provide.

Talking of which, the first place we came to on the beach was the Paradise Restaurant. This particularly interested Kevin because it served baked beans, something neither of us had seen since leaving England. It also offered FREED SHARK, SCAMBLED EGGS and LONG LIFE WITH TOMATO.

While he waited for his beans, Kevin told me his experience back at Arsikere station, while on the train to Londa. He had been woken at 4 in the morning by a loud squeaking from somewhere out on the dark platform. Looking out of the window, he had seen the strangest thing – a cartload of giant pigs, taking turns at being picked up by their ears (and *only* their ears) and loaded onto the backs of porters. Kevin said that the sight of all these squeaking hundred-pound pigs being hoisted into the air by their ears was the weirdest thing he'd seen in India so far.

February 28th

While everybody else in Colva retired for a three-hour siesta, Kevin and I braved the intense heat in the open and travelled via Panjim to the small town of Old Goa.

Here, in the massive Professed House and Basilica of Bom

Jesus, reposes a small silver casket containing what remains of St Francis Xavier's remains. On special holy days, the box makes a special tour round town in a big procession. These are popular times for fanatic worshippers to make off with yet more of the dead saint's bones. One of them, we learnt, had already succeeded in absconding with his entrails!

Moving on to the Convent and Church of St Francis of Assisi, we noted it badly in need of renovation but still possessed of stunning 16th century woodwork and murals. It also had a museum full of portraits of ex-Viceroys from Portugal. Every one of them looked extremely depressed. They evidently had not relished their appointment to India at all.

Our last stop, the Se Cathedral, was the largest church I had seen since St Peter's in Rome. We spent hours exploring its endless dark corridors, its long, winding stone staircases, and its small, deserted study-rooms, often full of dusty old manuscripts and cobwebs. Eventually, however, the continuing eerie echo of our lonely footsteps up and down the gloomy corridors, together with the dead building's musty odour of damp decay, filled us both with a heavy sense of unease and we hurried back into the warm light of day.

Kevin suggested I might care to see the cathedral's famous 'Golden Bell' before leaving. He politely indicated an open side-door which led the way up. Thanking him for his consideration, I began my ascent. Halfway up, however, I noticed stair-boards missing. And as I neared the top, the stair-boards that were left began to crumble beneath my feet. Having now nearly fallen down the high bell-tower to my death, I decided to check things out with Kevin. Was he sure, I shouted down, that this bell was open to the public? A moment later, his response floated up. Well no, it wasn't, he hollered but he had felt so sure that I would want to see the Bell that he'd picked the locked entrance door just to let me in. I shouted down that if I made it back to the bottom alive, I should reward his thoughtfulness by wringing his neck.

March 1st

They say that on Colva Beach you can, if you walk far enough, find somewhere to be quite alone, somewhere where nobody and nothing will disturb you. Many travellers insist that this is the only place in India where this is possible.

Walking down the silky sands in search of *my* private 'place in the sun', I came across Martin, a friend I had made back in Mysore. He too was trying to be alone. Martin looked rather glum, so I sat down to share a cigarette with him and asked him why. He told me a very odd story, about his bus journey up to Goa a few days back. He had been sitting on the bus, minding his own business, when a very beautiful Indian woman had settled next to him. This in itself was strange, for women in this country were brought up to eschew the company of men until properly introduced. But what happened next was even more of a surprise. The woman had started winking at him, and then moved her hand off her lap to massage his knees, then his private parts. It was dark and nobody else on the bus could see what was happening. Martin knew what was happening, and couldn't believe it. He was even more astounded when the woman leant over to suggest they take a private room together that night in Goa. The rest of the journey passed with him in a positive lather of anticipation.

Arriving at Goa, he quickly scooped his bags up and moved to follow the dusky beauty out of the bus. But then he reached the door and, looking down, received a nasty shock. His precious pearl of the East had just been set into a ring of waiting relatives! Somehow, they had got wind of her heading their way and had come to the bus-station to pick her up. Poor Martin, he still hadn't got over it.

About two miles down the beach, I finally found my quiet spot. My only companions, for as far as the eye could travel, were the gaunt skeletons of a few old fishing boats. Oh, and of course the seagulls. These light, graceful birds settled like butterflies along the water's edge, pausing only moments at a time on the sands before soaring off into the air again in a sudden flurry of wings and feathers. Otherwise, apart from the scuttle of tiny sea-crabs running before the incoming surf, the whole scene was a poem of peace.

My only activity today was a walk up to the charming village of Benaulim, set back from the beach. On the way, I stopped for a drink at Pedro's Restaurant. The waiter here offered me something called 'heaven flower' which wasn't on the menu at all. It turned out to be a popular local brand of hashish. I just told him I couldn't afford it. But this only encouraged him. He offered me a job in the restaurant. That way, he suggested, I could *make* the money to afford it!

March 2nd

I walked down the beach this morning to see the sun rise. This time, as it was very early, I did not have to walk far to find a secluded spot. First I squatted down in some bushes behind a palm-tree alcove to complete my morning toilet, and then I sat down in the sand to begin my morning prayers.

I had barely started when an odd snorting, snuffling sound behind me drew my attention. Whirling round in alarm, I saw a large wild pig rooting around in the bushes. It was eagerly devouring my exuded faeces. So the infamous Goan pigs had caught me up at last! And this wasn't the end of it. Turning back to face the dawn, I noticed a small flea-ridden puppy-dog dragging itself up the beach toward me. It arrived, and lay panting at my feet, gazing up at me with a look of happy devotion. Then it began nibbling my toes. How I managed to keep my mind on the Mystic Law of life and finish my prayers, I'll never know.

There was a sprightly wind in the air today, and my last swim in Colva's warm waters was enlivened by the arrival of a series of powerful, driving waves, which produced an invigorating strong current. The sun remained just the same, however – intense and very hot. I was most loath to leave.

But the time had come to move on. Kevin and I packed our bags, and prepared to journey up to Poona. It would be the last time that we would be travelling together – at least for the time being. But it was not the thought of solo travel that concerned us most today. It was, rather, the prospect of yet another long train journey. We both boarded the 12.35pm train from Margao station with sinking hearts.

I spent the first few hours of the journey in a state of depression, listening to Frank Sinatra on tape singing all about how alone he was without a friend in the world. Only when we reached Ghathbratha station did things finally liven up. It was here that the train began loading on a shipment of *thali* suppers for its passengers. Chapatis, idlis, cucumbers, curd and masala chips were flying about all over the place. Everyone in our carriage had just about settled down to their meals, when a pair of scabrous mongrels began having a fight under our wheels. Their *thalis* abandoned, all the Indian passengers craned out of the windows to place loud bets on the outcome of this canine carve-up.

Kevin went up the platform for a cup of tea, and nearly got arrested over a two-rupee note. It was all he had, and the cha-boy had no change for it. The note passed back and forth rapidly between them, and then mysteriously disappeared. Kevin accused the cha-boy of having it and strode off with his cup of tea. The cha-boy accused Kevin of having it, and gave loud, hysterical pursuit. 'Thief! Thief!' he hollered, and the usual Indian crowd gathered to see what was going on. They quickly passed judgement against Kevin, and set the police on him. By the time he had talked his way out of this one, he was quivering with rage. I had never seen Kevin so overwrought. He sat back in his seat like a stone, and didn't utter a word for hours afterwards.

Despite all this fuss, and despite frequent delays, the train contrived to arrive in Poona an hour early. That was good. But it was now 3 in the morning, and we couldn't see how we were going to find any beds to sleep in. That was bad. But then a helpful cabbie turned up and drove us to the Kamlesh Tourist Lodge, which had rooms. That was good. Except that our room had a bowl-type toilet you couldn't sit on – there was nowhere for your legs to go. And that *was* bad. We had a comfortable bed each, which was very good, but they proved *too* comfortable and that was downright frustrating! After weeks of sleeping on hard planks, bruising bus seats, spartan train bunks, filthy thin mattresses or simply on the bare ground itself, a foam-filled luxury bed like this gave us real problems. I hardly slept a wink all night.

March 3rd

Preparing to set off alone tomorrow, I went down this morning to Poona station to book a train ticket to Aurangabad. It was here that I came up against one of those ghastly train reservation queues that tourists tell such chilling tales about. I had managed to avoid them so far, but the moment I entered the busy station I knew my number was up.

Before I was allowed to join the massive queue for tickets, I had to get a 'reservation slip'. But the clerk I approached for this had just run out of them. While awaiting the arrival of a fresh supply, he went off for a long tea break. I only got the reservation slip an hour later. And I still couldn't join the ticket queue – I had to get the slip 'number stamped' by the platform ticket collector. This was a very elusive gentleman who, when I finally tracked him down, didn't speak a word of English. But I got my slip stamped and at last joined the ticket queue. It stretched like a long, winding snake out of the large station concourse and into the street. The Indian in front of me at the rear of the queue turned round to look at the number on my ticket, and just laughed. He told me not to bother queuing up at all – I wouldn't be getting my ticket until sometime in the middle of next week.

Fortunately, I met Ram. Or rather – as is generally the case – Ram attached himself to me. He was a seedy, lank-haired, depressed individual who seemed to be carrying the whole weight of the world around on his hunched shoulders. He introduced himself to me with the faintest flicker of a grin and, taking a look at my reservation slip, told me that there was no problem – I should go away now and wander round town with him for a while. If I came back in three hours, he assured me, my number would certainly be called and I should be able to walk right to the front of the queue.

I decided to trust him and we walked along together to meet Kevin. Kevin gave Ram a look of no confidence, and asked him if he was happy. Ram said he would only be happy when he had enough money. He soon dropped his pretence of being a 'genuine tourist guide', and began asking us if we had any American dollars to sell. To keep us sweet, he stopped at a nearby sugar-cane press on the roadside, and bought us two large glasses of frothy yellow cane juice. This was *too* sweet, however, and Kevin gave his to an elderly beggar, who gulped it down eagerly. We later learnt that this juice – pressed from unwashed canes grown in fields 'fertilised' with human excrement – was one of the biggest causes of amoebic dysentery in Poona.

The day ended well, though. I returned to the station concourse three hours later to find that my number had just been called. The milling crowd round the ticket window immediately let me through to make my purchase. It was just as Ram had predicted.

Part Three

Buddha and the Bodhi Tree

March 4th

I woke this morning to find Kevin back at the mirror, polishing his bald head with fanatic zeal. He was determined to get his hair back as soon as possible. I told him that if he rubbed it hard enough, he might get three wishes. In which case, he could make a full head of hair one of them.

As I waved farewell to Kevin from the early bus to Aurangabad, I briefly wondered how I would do without his infectious good humour and enthusiasm. But two months is a long time to travel with someone, and both of us by now needed to discover how we would cope on our own. I turned to locate my reserved seat in the packed bus, and instantly forgot all about Kevin. There was a stubborn old man in my seat. It took me ages to persuade him out of it.

Soon after that, the heat hit me. As we plunged inland, the fierce desert breeze blew in through the open windows and dried me out to a withered husk. At each (infrequent) stop the bus made, I was forced to down several glasses of the only cold beverage on sale: sugar-cane juice. As we progressed, the landscape grew ever more dry and barren. The baked desert, scorched white by the sun, shimmered with such intense brilliance that my eyes were constantly smarting and red. And all that I could see, through the thick clouds of dust blowing up from the parched dirt-track, was an endless terrain of flat plains, arid wasteland and burnt-ochre foothills. The only people I saw the whole six hour journey were two brave souls marching purposefully off into the heart of the bleached wilderness – both looking buoyantly optimistic. What about, I couldn't hazard a guess. There was nothing, absolutely *nothing,* out there!

At Aurangabad, I took a clean dormitory bed in the Youth Hostel, which also provided a TV lounge, a restaurant and recreational facilities, and a mosquito net – all for just six rupees (50 pence) per night. It was a real find!

Aurangabad itself was a quiet, sleepy town, full of unemployed rickshaw drivers, diffident beggars, and lazy sugar-cane stands doing little or no business at all. The general atmosphere of the place was extremely laidback. Which was exactly what I needed as I adjusted to travelling alone in this unpredictable country, and after such a long and tiring bus journey.

March 5th

The road out from Aurangabad throws a sharp right turn towards Ellora, just as you leave town. This turning is marked by a grotesque monument in the road, constructed from what looks like bright-blue bicycle wheels. Taking a cheap bus tour to the Ellora Caves this morning, this odd signpost was the only thing with any colour in it I saw all day.

Despite a certain stark beauty, the scenery outside the bus was uniformly drab. All we saw for miles were bleak flat-top mountains gasping in the heat of a brush-strewn empty desert. The only variation to this were the few rows of banyan trees which occasionally appeared by the roadside. They were the largest and oldest ones I had yet seen, and by far the thirstiest!

Their drooping branches threw out long tendrils which scraped vainly for moisture in the dry dust like bony, desiccated fingers. All of us on the bus knew how they felt – by the time we made our first stop, at Daulatabad, our mouths and throats felt dry as parchment.

Daulatabad is a deserted hilltop fortress, the only raised point in the middle of a flat, uninhabited wilderness. It is the creation of the mad Muhammed Tughlaq, who some centuries ago decided to move his capital here from Delhi. Paranoically concerned about security, he erected a remarkable seven-walled fort here atop a massive rock outcrop: even its battlements had battlements! The many mighty wooden gates had been spiked to deter elephant charges, the surrounding moat had been populated with crocodiles, and the whole fortress was full of dead-end ambush points, hidden firing hoes and boiling-oil channels to overwhelm any invading force. Despite all these inventive defences, however, Daulatabad had spent most of its active life being captured! Using typical Indian guile, the invaders hadn't bothered fighting through all those tiresome defences – they had simply bribed the guards to let them in the front gate.

Muhammed had tired of being invaded after a while, and seventeen years after arriving had marched all his subjects back north again. Thousands of them had perished on the journey down, thousands more had died of thirst and boredom in Daulatabad itself, and most of the remainder expired on the long trek back to Delhi. In just twenty years, Muhammed Tughlaq had achieved the nearest thing to mass genocide in the India of his day.

At Grisheshwar, site of one of twelve ancient Shiva *jyotolingas* (stone penises), I tried to enter the inner shrine but was stopped by a frowning priest. He showed me to a sign which

123

said: 'Visitors wishing to achieve *dharvana* with the Deity must Take off Their Clothes'. I shook my head and moved on. Nobody was going to get me to strip off for a stone phallus.

By the time we drew near to Ellora, the heat had become unbearable. It was so bad that a lone banyan tree I saw in the desert had no less than thirty bullocks crowded beneath its flimsy shade. They all looked exactly how I felt – damnably hot and thirsty.

We came down from an enjoyable tour of the Ellora Caves to a small roadside restaurant. My 'lunch' here was five consecutive cups of tea, the sun having reached unbelievable intensity. I gasped away in the shade, and watched an itinerant cow wander in from off the street. First it gobbled down a dirty old newspaper by my feet, then it ambled off and began experimentally nibbling at a small child sitting in the dust. The child only just escaped.

The tour over, I took supper this evening at Pinky's Restaurant in Station Road. Its advertisement of 'beer permit' was irresistible. 'Do come inside, sir,' requested the friendly manager. 'We cannot serve alcohol outside – today is a "dry" day.' I told him he wasn't joking, and entered. Then I sampled his menu. I liked the sound of FRIED FISH WITH CHEEPS, and of MASH ROOM WITH BOOMBOO HOOTS. But ASSORTED OLD MEATS and CHICKEN ANTIQUE didn't appeal in the slightest. As for the manager he was far too busy trying to buy my solar-powered pocket calculator to trouble himself with taking my order. So I stuck with the beer.

March 6th

After a good night's sleep up on the hostel roof (the steamy dorm below was like the Black Hole of Calcutta), I determined to explore the nearby Aurangabad Caves and took a long rickshaw ride into the middle of the desert to see them.

As at Ellora, these caves had been chiselled into the side of a mountainside cleft. Looking down, the desert plains panned out in a vast, sweeping expanse, the monotony broken only by the tiny glittering city of Aurangabad below. I viewed all this with awe tinged with anxiety – this was all very pretty, but would I have enough water to get back alive? Summer had come early to Aurangabad this year. At least two months early. The plains below were stricken pale and dumb by the unrelenting blast of the noonday sun. I hurried into the caves, eager for their cool shade.

There were ten of them in all – grey inner shrines containing Buddhas, bodhissatvas and lesser deities, all superbly carved into the rock. And they charted the rise and fall of Buddhism in this region – the first two caves having nothing but a large simple Buddha inside (seated), while the next three had him 'guarded' by not-so-Buddhist thugs waving clubs or 'attended' by large-breasted erotic dancers. How the Buddha kept his mind on his enlightened condition, I can't imagine! By the time they constructed Cave Six, the monks had begun to favour Brahmanism again, so that statues of Shiva, Ganesh and other Hindu gods share equal billing with those of the Buddha. This theme continued into Cave Seven, which had the most beautiful carvings of all. I came to this cave to find it being cleaned and renovated by a crew of noisy, friendly workmen. I asked them how they had got up to this desolate spot today, and they pointed to Cave Eight, which they had just turned into a bicycle shed.

Unable to see a rickshaw anywhere, I decided – even though my water-bottle was now empty – to walk down off the

mountain and over the sun-baked desert by foot. This turned
out to be a relatively pleasant excursion. Despite a raging
thirst, I took comfort from the bleak but majestic views along
the descent, and found the solitude of this walk most welcome.
It was the only the second time (after Colva Beach) I had been
truly alone in India.

Half an hour later, I staggered into a small shanty town,
populated by large numbers of dirty, noisy children. 'Goodbye!
Goodbye!' they shouted at me as I approached. What a strange
greeting, I thought. Surely they meant 'Hello!' But no, they
knew exactly what they meant. They had seen what I had just
seen – a pack of heat-maddened wild dogs bolting down the
road, intent on ripping me to shreds.

It is incredible how fast one can run when one has to.

Exhausted, I took a rickshaw the rest of the way home.
Then, at 7.30pm, I commenced the long trip back to New
Delhi, taking the bus for Manmad.

At Manmad station I began what was to be the most harrowing night of my life. The ordeal started with a gang of local
youths lobbing a succession of paper cups at my bald head on
the platform. Before I could object, they had run off into the
darkness, giggling like a pack of naughty schoolboys. Fuming
with annoyance, I realised – for the first time since leaving
Kevin – the worst drawback of travelling alone. Bad experiences, instead of being laughed off with a companion, simply
fester away inside and turn sour.

My train was two hours late in arriving, which didn't help
matters. And then, the final disaster, I couldn't find the sleeping berth I had reserved. I studied the carriage and berth numbers on my ticket, and found what I thought must be my bunk.
But there was an Indian already asleep in it. He stirred himself
to look at my ticket and told me I was in the wrong carriage.

I'll never know why I believed him, but I did. Several frantic enquiries on the platform got me nowhere. Then, as the train began to move out of the station, an impatient rail official bustled me into the nearest carriage and told me not to worry. But I did worry. This carriage was choc-a-bloc full of soldiers, beggars and destitutes. There was hardly room to stand, let alone sit down.

Sandwiched between sweaty bodies, I seethed with frustration as I waited to put matters straight at the next station. Coming into Jalgaon a long hour later, I struggled off the train and angrily demanded that the ticket collector confirm me in my correct sleeping berth. I told him that some shiftless scoundrel was already sleeping in it. That didn't go down too well. He shrugged and told me to sleep anywhere I could find. So I did. I spent the whole night hunched up under a dirty wash-hand basin next to the carriage toilet.

March 7th

I was jarred out of my fitful doze by a troop of noisy Indians trampling over me on their way off the train for breakfast. Casting a bleary eye outside, I saw that we had come to Itarsi. The busy, bustling platform was alive with ringing cries of 'Chai-*ya!*' and 'Om-e-*lette!*' And of course with the familiar racket of passengers giving their teeth some spit and polish at the platform double-sinks.

I was stiff and tired. After making an imaginary award to the most enterprising animal on the platform – a holy cow who had lifted an entire *thali* breakfast out of a passenger's hands (through a carriage window) with its long tongue – I finally found my correct seat. The cunning Indian who had 'borrowed' it last night had wisely made himself scarce. But if I thought my problems now over, I was mistaken. By the time we came to Bhopal, I had become besieged by a 28-yer old research scientist from Bihar. He was rich, unmarried and un-ashamedly homosexual. He was also surrounded by lots of grinning friends, which made being rude to him very inadvis-able. After a long hour of being winked at and having my leg stroked, however, I decided that enough was enough and fled up to my top bunk in full retreat. He spent the next *four hours* trying to coax me down again, gazing up at me with warm, wet, imploring eyes. That look will haunt my dreams for years to come!

Eventually, he was overcome by the heat and fell asleep. Which was my cue to creep off the train for my first cup of tea of the day. But my luck was out again. The cha-man on the platform seemed blind to my existence. He served the seven-teen Indian passengers behind me first, and then (and only then) did he give me a cup. I had just turned to drink it when I saw the train slipping noiselessly out of the station. Dropping the hard-fought-for cup of tea, I ran after it and leapt onto the last departing carriage.

I arrived in New Delhi at 9pm surly and tired, very anxious to find a bed for the night. A beaming rickshaw driver ran up to me, but I was in such a state that I just bared my teeth at him and defied him to overcharge me. 'No, no!' he placated me. 'There is no problem with fare – you name your own price!' Deflated, I let him drive me to the Hotel Chanakya in Market Street. The room I got here was so clean and quiet, that I gave him a very good price indeed. He deserved it.

I had a hot shower, ate a good meal, and sent my filthy laundry out to the dhobi. Then I felt almost human again. Sleep came the moment I hit the sheets.

March 9ᵗʰ

Continual travel through India requires a great deal of stamina. Waking up this morning, unable to move, I realised that I had just about run out of mine. The temptation to convalesce a further day in my hotel room was very great indeed. Nevertheless, I overcame it – I decided to visit New Delhi's famous Rail Transport Museum.

This was a happy decision. This charming little museum is quite a job to get to – it lies right at the edge of town, near the diplomatic enclave by Satya Marg – but more than repays one's effort. The best thing about it is not the small museum building itself, but the mock railway siding erected round it. This has one of the finest collections of old railway engines, wagons and carriages in the world. It even has a small 'toy train' track running round the complex, which undertakes regular trips for children. For young or old, this place is a perfect delight.

To get the best all-round view of the exhibition grounds, I climbed a small hump-back bridge at the back of the siding. From here, I could count over twenty assorted engines – old and new, steam and diesel, broad and narrow gauge – all of them immaculately maintained and set among beautiful green lawns and gardens.

Inside the actual museum, the most interesting exhibit I saw was the skull of a massive bull elephant which charged a train bound for Calcutta in 1894, and lost. It derailed the train and seven carriages, but plummeted to its death down a steep ditch. Both tusks were missing from the skull. One had been kept by the engine driver; the other had passed to the British Museum in London.

On the way home, I saw a very odd thing. Two young Indian cyclists collided with each other in the middle of a busy highway. Picking themselves up, they noticed that one of their bicycles had suffered serious damage – its front wheel was impossibly twisted. The youth with the undamaged bike thought about how to make amends. Then inspiration seized him, and he laid the bent wheel flat on the ground and began leaping up and down on it, trying to straighten it out in the middle of all the speeding traffic. A crowd gathered by the roadside to urge him on in this strange activity. Then, as both cyclists completed the 'repair' and wobbled off into the sunset, their audience gave a rousing cheer of applause.

Having returned to my hotel, I looked ahead to my forth-coming expedition into the 'holy' state of Bihar with very mixed feelings. The lure of the Buddha's land was strong, but the prospect of yet another marathon train journey filled me with dread. One more day of rest, I felt, would have made all the difference. But I was now racing against the clock – only five short days remained before I was due to reconnect with Kevin in Varanasi.

I mounted the evening train to Patna with serious misgiv-ings. But then I took a deep breath and plunged into the gloomy, noisy carriages determined to make the best of things. And on this occasion, fortune did smile on me. I found myself sharing a carriage with two charming young Japanese Bud-dhists – Kazuhisa Tanaka and Yasushi Imamura. Both young men were eager, friendly conversationalists, and the long jour-ney passed a good deal quicker for their warm, enjoyable company. I asked Yasushi why his clothes were splattered with green and red paint. He told that yesterday had been another 'Holi' festival day, and he had been showered with coloured water and powder from head to toe. Far from minding this rude treatment, he had so enjoyed himself gathering these 'battle scars' that he was taking these stained clothes home unwashed to show all his friends and relatives in Japan.

At one station along the route, an old beggar woman – her fingers eaten away by leprosy – thrust her stunted hands through the window begging for money. Taking a tip from Kevin, I decided to give her food instead, and passed through a small bunch of bananas.

Sleep came slow tonight. Two passengers without bunk reservations sat down on the edge of my berth and held a loud conversation until the lights went out. But I was lucky. The two Japanese had a much worse problem. They were in the top bunks, and the powerful ventilator fan over their heads couldn't be turned off. Blasted by the gusty draught throughout the night, they both woke up in the morning with stinking colds.

March 10th

I woke up this morning with two *different* passengers holding a loud conversation on the end of my bunk. I gritted my teeth, did some chanting to respect their lives, and gave them a death's mask grin of friendship. They returned my smile and gave me a cheery little wave. Later, they bought me a bag of peanuts.

In Patna, I booked a quiet but grubby room at the Hotel Gaylord. I asked the elderly proprietor five times for some fresh linen, then gave up and drifted off into a long sleep. Later, when it had become dark, I walked round the local neighbourhood in search of a good film. But there wasn't one to be found. The dimmed backstreets and alleyways positively seethed with disreputable ruffians and blackguards, all grinning out at me with appropriating eyes. I later learnt that Patna is notorious for its heavy population of thieves and vagrants. One of these days, I determined, I must get this kind of information in advance, rather than in retrospect. As it was, I picked my way back to the civilised part of town through the poorly lit, badly surfaced, beggar-strewn and generally unsavoury streets with a nervous sense of impending disaster. I wasn't just imagining it – the air was thick with trouble.

Ever since I'd hit the streets of Patna this afternoon – the lonely wind howling up and down the dusty, deserted highways – I had been feeling uneasy about this place. It put me on edge, and had given me a nagging toothache. Even when I finally got my fresh linen (on the sixth attempt), I wasn't much happier. Indeed, Patna as a whole was disturbingly short on laughs.

March 11th

Today marked the culmination of my journeys to various Buddhist centres in India – I would be travelling down to Bodhgaya, to see the Bodhi Tree. This tree is said to be a direct descendant of the one the Buddha sat beneath when he gained enlightenment some 3000 years ago. Naturally grown from a sapling of the original *pipal* tree which came from Sri Lanka 2000 years ago, it lies on the western side of the Mahabodhi Temple in Bodhgaya. No other tree in human history has been the subject of such particular reverence.

The importance of my pilgrimage seemed to throw up a lot of unforeseen obstacles. The journey from Patna to Bodhgaya should have taken just four hours. In my case it took eight – mainly because I overslept and missed the early train out of

Gaya. Two wasted hours were spent on Patna platform drinking innumerable cups of tea and fending off friendly beggars.

The later train to Gaya was jam-packed with people, stopped a total of fourteen times in between stations, and crawled into its destination two hours late. Walking out of Gaya station, I found a scene of absolute chaos. Struggling though a human sea of traders, passengers and beggars, I scanned the forecourt for an auto-rickshaw. With the town's bus station miles away at the other side of town, this was the only way I could see myself getting to Bodhgaya – thirteen kilometres down the road – tonight. But there *were* no auto-rickshaws, and no taxis either. Gaya appeared to be the one place in all India which didn't have them.

I was stumbling towards the distant bus station, weighed down with a heavy rucksack, when a voice floated over to me. 'You are wanting to go somewhere?' it offered. I looked up and saw an auto-rickshaw. I reached over and touched the driver's arm, just to make sure he wasn't a mirage. Then I gratefully accepted a ride. I offered him all that I had – twenty rupees – for the trip to Bodhgaya. But he wanted double. When I couldn't pay it, he went all round town collecting extra fares. By the time he had finished, the small five-seater vehicle was groaning beneath the weight of an astonishing *fourteen* passengers. I spent the whole journey bent double, with a suitcase on my head.

I got out at Bodhgaya feeling as though I'd just been run over by a truck. Curtly informing the rickshaw man that I had deducted eighteen rupees 'inconvenience tax' from his fare, I gave him just two rupees – like all the rest of his passengers. To my surprise, he didn't complain.

It was now near dusk, and the mosquitoes were already emerging from their little coffins and gathering hungrily around my unprotected flesh. It was vital that I find accommodation as soon as possible. But this, too, proved difficult. I dragged a poor cycle-rickshaw man all around town, trying various lodges and temples for a bed, but all were full. It was quite dark when we reached the Burmese Monastery and my long search finally came to an end. The room I obtained here was the cheapest I'd had yet (Rs3), but was little more than a bare prison cell. Apart from a crumbling table and chair, there was no furniture. The 'window' was a hole in the wall. The bed was single bare board, raised from the floor on a few bricks. There was no mattress or linen on it. Neither was there any ventilating fan, and the close evening air lay like a thick blanket over the room. But of course, there were plenty of mosquitoes! By the dim light of the single bare bulb, I could see them swarming in through the hole in the wall. They looked very pleased to see me. 'Well, hello there!' they seemed to be saying. 'Mind if we drop in for a bite of supper?' And there was no denying them.

But at least I had reached my objective. Taking up my book and beads, I went up to the Mahabodhi Temple. It was quiet here, but still open for business. Coming to the main shrine, I asked the shaven-headed monk on duty whether I could pay my respects to the Lord Buddha. He nodded, and asked another monk to be my escort. We went in silence round the side of the temple and turned a corner. Suddenly, there it was – the Bodhi Tree.

It stood inside a small stone pavilion, and was quite deserted. All those difficulties I had experienced in coming here turned out to be a benefit – nobody came out *this* late in the evening (9pm) to pay their devotions. I would be able to pray quite alone.

Or so I thought. My yellow-robed guide had retired into the

night after letting me through the pavilion, and I had thought him gone. But then, as I settled beneath the Bodhi Tree and prepared to begin my prayers, he suddenly reappeared. Wild-eyed and excitable, the agitated young monk dashed over to tell me I was committing heresy, and began insisting I chant *his* mantra. It was after only a long comparison of the relative merits of our separate Buddhist faiths that he finally relented and sloped back off into the darkness.

I was now at last free to relax and enjoy my devotions. Seated within the embrace of the holy tree, I was conscious that it was here – three thousand long years ago – that the original Buddha had sat also, summoning forth the natural wisdom and life-force of this mighty *pipal* tree to set down the roots of a whole new religion for mankind. It also crossed my mind that he had endured many difficult hardships before coming to this place of his enlightenment, which surely (albeit in microcosm) reflected my own situation today.

March 12th

Had I known even *half* of what was coming my way today, I would never have got out of bed. It started quietly enough, back at the Bodhi Tree for morning prayers. The gnarled old sweeper attending the enclosure gave me a kind gift of dried leaves from the tree to take home as keepsakes. Thanking him, I stood back to view the stately, dignified bower at leisure. It was covered with tiny coloured flags and streamers, and was full of birds. The whole temple complex was thronged with birds, but they only seemed to alight and sing on this one tree.

As I walked the temple grounds, I passed along the famous 'Jewel Walk' and sat by the beautiful Lotus Pond. Later, in between the many small devotional *stupas* (stone shrines) erected privately round the temple circumference, I watched Buddhist devotees (of some ascetic sect) sliding back and forth on wooden prayer boards, their hands enclosed in small protective gloves to guard against friction burns and splinters. Finally, I came to the large golden statue of the Buddha within the main temple shrine. It was quite magnificent. Only one thing concerned me – the preponderance of money boxes in this place of worship. Also, there was the urchin who dragged me to see a crumbling bit of stone which he assured me was 'Buddha's mother'. He asked for money, too.

Near the Mahabodhi Temple is the Tibetan Monastery, housing the 'Wheel of Law'. This 'wheel' – housed in a richly decorated and painted chamber – is actually a huge metal drum about thirty feet high. The inscription reads:

It is Wheel of Law. It is full of millions of hymns of Shree Vajrasattva and others deities. Please turn it once or twice from left to right. It is for the neollence of human being and cures the sins. It weigh more than 200 quentals.

I entered to find a small monk revolving the wheel slowly, ringing a little bell repeatedly as he walked around. He told me that if I joined him and went three times round in an anti-clockwise direction, all my past sins would be forgiven. I turned the wheel hopefully.

Back in my primitive cell, I considered whether or not to stay another night in Bodhgaya. Suddenly, my mind was made up for me. A huge, furry tarantula climbed in through the window, and began dashing round the room gobbling up mosquitoes. Before it moved on to me, I made a dash for my bags. I was fully packed and out of the Burmese Monastery in two minutes flat. You don't see a lot of spiders in this country, but when you do, they are *enormous*. And they move very fast.

I left Bodhgaya at 9pm, and soon regretted it. To start with, the bus to Gaya had 77 passengers on board. I spent the whole trip wishing I had been born a dwarf. Then, in Gaya, I was told to wait at a bus-stop for the connection on to Nalanda. The 'bus-stop' was nothing more than a crowded cesspit on the side of the road, in which two crows were pecking out the eyes of a dead dog.

The bone-crunching bus journey to Nalanda left my backside red-raw and aching. It was so bad that the bumpy tonga-ride up to the ruins of the (famous) Buddhist university had me weeping into my rucksack. I only raised my head to admonish the driver for whipping his poor old donkey on with a split bamboo cane.

My plans to stay at Nalanda this night were rudely destroyed. The only tourist accommodation I found – the Burmese Rest House – wanted an extortionate twenty rupees even to sleep on the roof. I decided to take a chance on getting back to Patna tonight instead.

This meant I had to move fast. After a rapid whistle-stop tour of the area – walking quickly round this ancient seat of Buddhist learning (and site of the oldest university in the world) – I returned to the waiting tonga. The driver took me back to the bus-stop without inflicting any more wounds on the exhausted donkey, and I boarded the midnight bus for Bihar Sharif. This had a record number of passengers – eighty-two in all, plus an extra contingent on the roof. The only advantage of standing the whole journey was that my backside (now quite numb with pain) was spared further damage.

But then came the final leg. The three-hour bus trip back to Patna, and this was a quite unforgettable experience. I thought at first I had been lucky to secure a seat on the roof (the inside of the bus was jammed solid with people), for the heat and dust would have made travelling below like standing in a moving coffin. As soon as the bus started, however, I changed my mind. It set off down the highway as if pursued by the Devil himself. The ensuing blast of wind, dust and insects nearly blew me off the roof. Recovering my balance, I looked round and noticed that I was sharing this precarious situation with twenty-five flint-eyed Bihar bandits. They all swore a lot, stamped, clapped and sang raucously, in between surveying me coldly when I didn't join in and fingering my bags with covetous intent. I became uncomfortable. I became even more uncomfortable when the sun's warm rays faded, and the biting night wind sprang up.

Halfway through the long, cold journey, the ugly gorillas sitting with me on the roof took a violent dislike to an Indian who had taken a seat down below without consulting them. They wanted that seat. All of them wanted it. They wanted it so badly that they stopped the bus five times within the next hour to argue the case. Eventually, the poor driver became so harassed that he chucked the interloping Indian off the bus and left him shivering on the cold, dark road in the middle of nowhere.

It was now quite dark. The wind was one long continuous icy gale. The ruffians on top snuggled up to me for warmth. I didn't dare object, lest they decided they didn't like me after all, and instead opted to toss me off the roof into the black, friendless night. I lay quietly on the roof in their midst, frozen to the bone, and wondering how it was possible for three short hours to seem like three endless days.

I arrived back in Patna in poor condition indeed. And the Hotel Gaylord, remembering the fuss I'd made about the fresh linen, conspired to give me the darkest, dingiest and dirtiest room they had. I didn't have to complain about the linen in this one – it didn't have any linen to complain about. I didn't wash, undress or unpack. I simply lay on the bare bed, and slept a solid nine hours.

March 13th

Today I prepared to leave the state of Bihar, on the midday train to Varanasi. Whilst not friendly, the station platform at Patna seethed with life and action. People busily unloaded bales of chopped wood, banana leaves and sugar-cane. Food vendors, selling handmade biscuits swarming with flies, loudly advertised their wares. Soldiers lay all over the place, looking disconsolate and bored. Beggars and cripples shuffled back and forth on box-carts, stretching their hands (when they had them) out for alms. Travellers coming off the train lay down to sleep on the platform, their clothes red and purple stained from Holi celebrations. Children ran up and down the platform, selling bananas and peanuts. In the background, a tinny tannoy blared out continuous unintelligible train directions. The whole scene was one large sprawling panorama of noise, colour and activity – a magic lantern of shifting images, moving through a choking backdrop of heat, pungent smells, and dust.

I was in no state for this last long train journey. Not only could I not remember my last solid meal, but my mind was now so disoriented by all the buses and trains I had been on recently that I could hardly remember where I was at present, let alone where I had come from or was going to. As I boarded the train, feeling vacant, an Indian enquired: 'Where are you coming from?' and I just couldn't tell him. Five long minutes passed. Then I gazed blankly at him and replied: 'Patna...I think.' There was no question about it. I was in a bad way.

It was during this final run into Varanasi that I finally lost all sense of time, space and feeling. I came to the end of it completely broken and beaten in mind, body and spirit. The crush to get on that train on the first place had taken my last reserves of strength. And there were so many bodies piled up around me inside, that I lay in the tiny prison of a top bunk for seven wearing hours, unable to move a muscle. Nobody around me spoke a word of English. But that was nothing new; ever since leaving Delhi, I hadn't met a soul who spoke my language. By now, I was so starved for conversation that I was beginning to hold discussions and debates with my tape recorder.

After a while, I got a grip on myself and told my mind to relax, and to trust that all would be well. And it was. As we came into Varanasi, my hold on reality and on my sanity was tenuous. But it was still there. I hailed a rickshaw driver, and told him to take me to a hotel, *any* hotel, that he could think of. He could only think of the Hotel Venus, a grubby, dirty establishment miles out of town. Again, I had a room with an overhead fan which blew all my clothes out the window. The small room-boy gave me an apologetic look. He had just fished out a pair of dirty underpants and soiled pyjamas from behind my bed.

Sitting at a nearby cafe, drinking ten consecutive cups of tea, I surveyed my condition. I felt incredibly old, incredibly dirty and incredibly tired. Over the past ten days I had covered more distance (3,000 kilometres) than Kevin and I had achieved in a whole month of regular travel. And much of it had been through the poorest, dirtiest and most perilous state in India – Bihar. All that I needed now was a good hot shower and a great deal of sleep. I was looking forward to meeting Kevin again tomorrow. I had a great deal to tell him.

Kevin and I in India

March 14th

Early this morning, a small wizened brown man appeared at my door. He broke wind repeatedly, and insisted on giving me a massage. Undeterred by my objections, he produced a book of 'testimonials' from previous satisfied customers, and began trying to knead the kinks out of my shoulders. I only ejected him with difficulty. He was remarkably strong.

After ten days travelling on my own, I was due to meet up with Kevin today at noon, outside Varanasi's Tourist Office in the Mall. As I drew up in my rickshaw, a familiar voice drifted over to me. 'Hello Baldy!' it cried. And there was Kevin – lying in the shade of a low wall by the tourist office. He looked very hot, and still very bald himself.

Pleased to see each other, we began exchanging our separate experiences. Kevin had quite a lot to tell me. After Poona, he had gone to Bombay. Most of his time there had been spent hiding in his hotel room, his only forays into the outside world being to grab the occasional meal. His first night in Bombay, he had strolled out into the dark street to get a cup of coffee, and had immediately been chased back inside by a pack of wild dogs.

The next day, there had been a big festival on (probably 'Holi') and gangs of laughing Indian youths had pelted him with red paint every time he came into sight. Surviving this ordeal, and having fought off masses of traders trying to buy his dollars or sell him drugs, he had come to the famous Taj Hotel. The contrast between its lush, luxurious interior, and the nearby encampment of homeless, casteless beggars living in sackcloth tents at the side of an open sewer-line, came as a shock.

Kevin's most interesting acquaintance in Bombay had been

a little old man who took him off to see the city's burning grounds. He told Kevin that if he waited long enough, the bodies burnt here reached such intense heat that the heads exploded with a loud pop, and the brains slid out. He had been genuinely puzzled that Kevin didn't want to see this, and had become quite affronted when he didn't go along with him to see the tower-tops where the Parsees put their dead out to be eaten by vultures.

Like most old men in India, this relic of the Raj proceeded to bore Kevin with countless stories of his glorious days in the British army. Then he had tried to show him the brothels of Bombay. He told Kevin that many girls came into these brothels after being kidnapped off the streets, and that they were kept in cages to prevent them escaping. Then he had asked Kevin for money, in return for this unsolicited (and unsavoury) guided tour of the city. Kevin had left Bombay in very sad spirits.

He had travelled on to Varanasi on a train packed to the ceiling with boisterous Indians. Within his small 6 x 6 feet compartment, he had counted 17 people. Every inch of space had part of a human body wedged into it. Every bunk he could see had three people on it – a) the person who had reserved it, and b) two squatters who hadn't even bought tickets. Each bunk was also occupied by a large heap of baggage. And each time the train stopped at a station, another crowd of people forced their way on. Kevin's principal concern was not, however, suffocation. What he had been really worried about was the periodic downfalls of urine coming from a small baby sandwiched in the bunk directly above his head.

Four long hours after leaving Bombay, the ticket collector had finally shown up to kick all the squatters off the train. Then all the doors to the train had been bolted shut, to stop any more getting on at future station stops.

Reaching Jalgaon, Kevin had looked out onto the platform to note a large black cow flopping down to sleep on top of a pile of beggars. They had seemed used to this kind of thing, for they didn't wake up. Kevin also noticed, near the entrance to this station, a pack of small black pigs busily engaged in eating cow dung. He had thought this rather strange. Though, having seen what the pigs got up to in Goa, he shouldn't really have been at all surprised.

He had broken his journey at Jalgaon, meaning to follow in my footsteps and visit the Buddhist caves at Ellora and Ajanta. But then he had had second thoughts. He'd suddenly remembered how fed up he'd become of caves and temples – he didn't want to see another one again, if he could help it. So he moved along that night to a small village nearby, called Bhusawal, and had a few beers to help him forget the close, suffocating heat, and to get some sleep.

The following morning, waiting for his train for Varanasi on Bhusawal station, Kevin spent an absorbing hour watching the behaviour of the local tribesmen, several of whom were apparently living on the platform, sharing an existence of dire poverty here with their animals. Smeared in dirt and excrement, and often wandering around completely naked, they reminded him of aborigines.

'One chap I saw,' he recalled, 'was really enjoying the company of his cows. He was stroking their noses and talking to them like children. And he was sharing his food with them – they were eating from the same plate as him. And when he'd finished, he scooped up a handful of cow's urine from off the platform and began washing his face with it. Another tribesman I noticed was sitting nearby with his legs wide open, playing with himself with a big smile on his face. This has to be the *weirdest* railway station I've ever been to!'

After a short rest, we went out to explore our surroundings. A rickshaw man with the unlikely name of 'Om' was lying in wait for us just outside the lodge. Om was a brush-haired, gap-toothed scoundrel who had a real way with words. He had got the psychology of working himself into tourists' good graces down to a fine art. He saw Kevin's mouth about to shape the words 'No thanks', and quickly intervened with an offer we couldn't refuse. 'Pay what you like!' he said. 'If you are happy, then I am happy!' What a reasonable proposition. Of course it made Kevin very happy indeed. Which was most unusual. He normally had such a stormy relationship with rickshaw drivers.

Om was of course out to make lots of money from us, but he tackled his task with such skill and dexterity that we couldn't but applaud his efforts. There was, for example, the huge public sitar and table music exhibition that he spent a whole hour persuading us to see. He really put his all into communicating his enthusiasm to us. By the time we got near the exhibition, he'd worked us up to such a lather of anticipation that we couldn't think of anything else on earth we'd rather see. Which was unfortunate, as it turned out. For it wasn't a public exhibition at all, and it wasn't (as Om claimed) free. He came to a stop outside a grimy old building down a narrow back alleyway, and showed us into a small private room containing jut one other occupant – a loquacious, heavily-bearded sitar player. This chap shook his head mournfully when we arrived, and apologised that the tabla-drum man was in hospital. Om withdrew discreetly from sight. Half an hour later, the sitar-man was still tuning up his instrument and waxing lyrical about how well he knew Ravi Shankar. It was only when we got up to leave that he proclaimed himself ready to play. And when he did play, he was very good.

After the performance, we located Om and told him we were ready to leave. He did not want to leave. The landlord had just passed him a full chilum-pipe of best hash, and Om was ready to relax. The very last thing we wanted, however, was a disorientated Om driving us back through Varanasi's chaotic traffic. Even in his right mind, he was one of the most reckless drivers we'd yet come across. We therefore dragged him away from his 'relaxation', and he sulked the whole drive home.

March 15th

I was startled into wakefulness at five this morning by a voice ringing out in the darkness of the room. 'You'll never believe this, Frank!' announced Kevin, 'but I've just dropped my new toilet roll down the loo!' What a vexing situation. Toilet rolls are horrendously expensive in India, and Kevin had contracted diarrhoea. He had got this by following the advice of an Indian friend he'd made called Mukul. Mukul had told Kevin that the local water, while unfiltered, was safe to drink. Mukul was constantly calling Kevin when he was out, and leaving urgent messages for him to call back. Maybe he was having second thoughts about that water advice, and was ringing to apologise.

It was fortunate that Kevin woke me so early, because we had booked a boat trip down the Ganges which required us to leave the hotel at 5.30am. We had to leave then because the sunrise comes early this time of year, and floating down the Ganges at sunrise is apparently a magical, unmissable experience for the foreign traveller in India.

Lots of other things floating down the Ganges were not half so magical. We had boarded a small rowing boat and were marvelling at the red, glowing orb of the sun rising over this holiest of rivers, when Kevin shook us out of our reverie by pointing to a couple of dead goats drifting past. Our guide told us that any animal that dies in the vicinity is simply tossed into the water. He then pointed out a small white cloth bundle on the side of the river's bank, and told us it was a dead baby. Along with smallpox victims and priests, babies aren't burnt on funeral pyres. Instead, they are wrapped in cloth, have a large rock tied to them, and are rowed out and dumped in the middle of the Ganges. The guide was most informative. He told us that they didn't burn priests because priests are gods, and they don't think it respectful to burn their gods.

Watching Varanasi's sequence of *ghats* (bathing steps) coming alive with the dawn was certainly a fascinating sight. As our boat rowed slowly by, we viewed many Hindu devotees taking their ritual baths before going back up to the riverside temples for morning prayer; also men and women alike beating their clothes clean on the stones with quite desperate ferocity. There were old men expectorating jets of red *paan* juice across the waters, while the young men on the ghat steps were engaged in athletic contortions and exercises as part of their religious devotions. Elsewhere, in amongst the press of temples and shrines dotting the water's edge, packs of wild dogs and pigs played and fought and rummaged around in the filth on the banks for food.

As we came to the main burning ghat, the Manikarnika, the guide told us apologetically that no bodies were being burnt this morning. He was sorry, but this was a slow time of year for funerals. Then he tried to recompense us for this 'disappointment' by pointing out boatloads of American tourists passing by. They were entirely surrounded by small rowboats full of insistent tradesmen trying to sell them tourist junk.

These tiny boats had tacked themselves onto the American craft with long hooks, and stuck there with leech-like tenacity. To complete the scene, a large boatload of fake *sadhus* (holy men) came up and blocked their bows, denying the Americans further passage unless they made a cash 'donation'.

Religion seemed to be real big business in this city, re-marked Kevin. Only the day before, he had visited a hotel in which every room was jam-packed with pilgrims. The rooms were bare and dirty, yet they were being let out at an extortion-ate price to poor people making a pilgrimage to this city. Entire family units of ten to fifteen people were crammed into each small room like sardines, the greed of the lodge owner turning their spiritual journey into a physical purgatory.

As our tour drew to a close, the guide pointed out some houseboats moored close to the banks. 'Hippies living there,' he remarked. 'Also many mosquitoes.' The dour tone of his voice suggested that he was not impressed by such Western residents. He later informed us that they spent most of their time taking morphine and other heavy drugs.

The tour ended with us passing a conga-line of American tourists (all wearing identical white shorts and carrying identi-cal yellow lunch-boxes) and coming out on the high balcony of an old house, which afforded a good view of Varanasi's fa-mous Golden Temple. Seeing this reminded me of Tim and Jill, whom we'd met in Ooty. They had put up at the Yogi Lodge, very near to the Golden Temple. They had been woken in the middle of the night by what sounded like the house next door being demolished. Peering sleepily out of their window, they discovered that the house next door *was* being demol-ished. An illegal demolition crew had assembled in the dead of night – to evade police detection – and were busily engaged in reducing this building to rubble with hammers, chisels, shovels and mallets. The next morning, there wasn't a stone left standing.

Back at the Garden View, we found Om waiting. How did he know we'd be there? Om was certainly living up to his name – not only omnipresent, but omniscient too. He took us to the State Bank in Varanasi's chaotic railway station. The main concourse inside the station was absolutely packed with sleeping or resting Indians. Most of them were there waiting for trains, or escaping from the fierce heat in the streets outside. There were flies everywhere. There was one dozing on the nose of the bank's security guard, who was also asleep. He sat outside the bank quite dead to the world, with his boots off and a double-barrelled shotgun propping up his chair.

Tonight we went to the cinema. There was a popular black and white Hindi picture showing. It was set in the Moghul era, the thin plot centring around the various struggles for power between exotically dressed and heavily bejewelled rajahs, princes and princesses.

The male lead started the ball rolling. He was middle-aged, extremely stout, and wore a look of impending tragedy on his noble features. Kevin, noting the huge helpings of rich, sumptuous food his part required him to eat, suggested that he was suffering a bad attack of wind. Either this, or he was trying to emulate the female lead, who was even more fat and grief-stricken than himself. Her high spot in the film came when she cantered up and down the palace battlements like a frisky elephant, singing a gaily pathetic song. The rajah, her father, had the good sense to haul her off the battlements and admonish her for making a spectacle of herself. His regal brows were creased in a deep frown throughout the picture. He had obviously read the script. His son, the rotund prince, laughed a lot in the wrong places. He had probably read the script, too.

The chaotic way in which the film had been edited suggested the work of either an irresponsible madman or an eccentric genius. It cut back and forth from one scene to another with frenetic, undisciplined energy, and no two consecutive scenes bore the slightest relation to one another. Kevin watched an hour of this in a state of suspended disbelief, and then fell asleep. He couldn't keep up with it.

March 16th

Breakfast was an event this morning. The waiter finally managed to bring in both our cheese omelettes and our chips at one and the same time. We gave him a rousing round of applause. Later, however, he blotted his copybook by serving up a plate of stale, bone-hard 'jam tost.' Kevin stabbed the toast with the desultory, hopeless air of one who never expects a good wholesome meal ever again. He spent the remainder of the morning writing a long letter to his parents, begging them to have a large plate of burnt sausages, roast chicken and crispy bacon waiting for him the moment he landed back in the UK.

Today we walked into town instead of hiring a rickshaw. Nearing the ghats, we suddenly left the busy, noisy part of Varanasi and plunged into the old city. This was in complete contrast, being a maze of quiet, winding backstreets and narrow lanes, overshadowed by tall, ancient buildings. It was very dark here, the towering old houses blotting out the sunlight to the cobbled street below. Nearly every corner we came to had small shops and stalls selling bangles and beads, curios and old coins, coloured scarves and fly-whisks. A few of them were even selling toy plastic motorboats, chugging aimlessly about in washing-up bowls. In this part of town, you could buy practically anything One enterprising Indian was even making a living from selling cow dung for fuel. His 'pitch' was just a short high wall, on which the neat little pats of poo had been arranged in a careful, artistic pattern.

Walking through the dark and crowded backstreets of the old city, we noticed large numbers of ownerless cows, dogs and goats wandering in and out of the many ruined buildings. As for the human population, this seemed to comprise mainly ragged old men, tiny naked children and badly crippled beggars. The streets were caked with excrement, and the air was musty and sweet with the odour of decay.

We emerged at last into the broad light of day again, having reached the site of the ghats. Each ghat had a long series of steps leading down into the Ganges. At regular intervals, teams of young lads would appear with powerful water-hoses to blast all the rubble and filth which had accumulated on the steps into the river. From the banks of the river itself came the constant calls of boat-boys wanting to take us to 'see the bodies burning'. This appeared to be the main tourist attraction.

Kevin really had it in for Indian salesmen today. Each time they came up to him offering to buy his dollars or take him to a silk factory, he glowered at them with undisguised loathing. One tout introduced himself as a 'fellow tourist', and pretended to be mortified when Kevin accused him of being 'just another bloody salesman!' He told us that 'Varanasi is a holy place, yes, but not everybody here is a holy man. I wish only to make friends with foreigners, not to sell them goods.' Kevin studied him with a cynical smirk, not believing a word of it, but allowed him to tag along after us. Sure enough, as we came to the edge of Manikarnika Ghat, this rascal's conversation began to drift from inconsequential small talk to his uncle's silk factory up the road...

I was just on the point of denouncing his treachery when an excellent photograph of the burning ghat presented itself. I stopped to size it up, allowing the others to move on ahead. What a mistake. No sooner had my camera clicked than I found myself in terrible trouble. An irate young Hindu appeared and began leaping up and down, shouting curses at me at the top of his voice. 'You take photo here? *Yes!*' he ranted. 'It is strict *forbidden*, take photo of holy burning ground! You come straight away, see my father who is policeman!' He continued in this fashion for some minutes, threatening to have my film destroyed and my camera dispossessed. I tried to explain that I didn't know, that nobody had told me photographs weren't allowed here, but he wasn't listening. He wasn't going to be satisfied with anything less than dragging me off to the nearest police station.

Or was he? Suddenly his frantic dance of rage petered out, and his stream of angry curses came to an end. He paused, and gave me an astonishing choice: 'Either you come now to police station,' he said, 'or you give me twenty rupees!'

I stared at him in disbelief. 'You mean,' I told him, 'that I have upset your gods by taking photo of your holy grounds, but that they will turn a blind eye to my offence if I pay you money? Don't be ridiculous!'

This response didn't please my assailant at all. He bared his teeth at me in a dangerous grin. 'You don't pay money, you try run away, my friends catch you, *make* you pay money!' he challenged. Darting a quick look behind him, I could see them collecting together and advancing ominously up the steps of the ghat towards us.

Suddenly, I thought of a way out. Rooting into my shoulder-bag, I withdrew my pocket cassette-recorder and waved it about in the young Hindu's face. 'Right!' I declared. 'I've taped everything you said! Including your attempt to extort money from me by force! *Now* we go to police station. Now *you* will be the one who will be in trouble!'

This desperate bluff had the gratifying effect of stopping the young thug dead in his tracks. The short pause it took him to figure out my deception was just long enough for me to beat a diplomatic retreat and vanish back into the safety of the nearby backstreets.

March 17th

After breakfast, we set out to explore Varanasi's old city and the ghats in more depth. Passing down a road fogged over by smoke from a road-asphalting works, we came out by a children's playground in which there were more goats than children. We went over the rail station bridge, noticing the great number of paan-splattered public spittoons erected here, and weaved in and out of the crowds of cows and bullocks taking their ease on the pavements or in the middle of the road.

Swallowed up once again in the warm, dark stomach of the old city, we fought our way through an army of one-armed, blind and legless cripples, and were eventually belched out on the site of Gai Ghat. From here, we had our best view yet of the stately Malviya Bridge. A short walk later, we reached Panchganga Ghat, and came across a grisly scene. At the foot of the ghat, occupying a wide expanse of grey-mud beach, a flock of giant vultures had gathered. They were busily engaged in dragging some human remains out of the river. This kind of thing is pretty common, particularly near the burning ghats, since few human bodies are entirely consumed by the flames of the funeral pyres. In the case of wealthy corpses, someone comes along to fold the head and legs into fire, ensuring a total cremation. In most other cases, however, these parts of the body are simply tossed into the Ganges, to be fed upon by dogs, pigs and vultures who patrol the water's edge in regular foraging parties.

As we watched in mixed fascination and horror, a small Indian boy appeared on a raised stone turret directly above the carrion birds and began lobbing large bricks and chunks of rubble down on them. One huge rock connected head-on with a vulture, dealing it a mighty blow. But it scarcely acknowledged this attack, for it made no attempt to fly away.

Past the impressive old walls and temples of Ram Ghat, we came once more to the burning grounds of Manikarnika Ghat. The whole area was dotted with high towers of wood and logs, which would be used to supply the funeral pyres. Before descending down into the ghat itself, we fortified ourselves with a 'Limca' lemon drink at a small backstreet shop to its rear. No sooner had we sat down than an eerie wail of human voices and musical instruments came into earshot. 'Sounds like a body,' remarked Kevin briefly. And he was right. Minutes later, a small band of flute and drum players came into view. They were followed by a small funeral bier on which a body rested, beneath a bright orange and red silk sheet. The sheet was covered with garlands of yellow flowers and a number of tiny red flags. The contrast between this noisy, colourful spectacle and the sombre, quiet and drab burial rituals of Western-style funerals struck us both. We decided to finish our drinks quickly, and follow on in the wake of the body to see what happened to it.

From the crest of the ghat, we observed the corpse's passage down the steps until it reached the water's edge. Here it was sanctified by shaven-headed priests, and its relatives and friends paid their last respects. I began to feel uncomfortable. I had the distinct feeling that I was being watched. Glancing suddenly to my right, I came eye to empty eye-socket with a charred human skull, grinning lifelessly at me from atop a nearby pyre. To my left, two new corpses had arrived, both wrapped in expensive silk shrouds. As we watched, these were covered very carefully with a number of wood logs, then sprinkled with perfumed wood chips and incense. After that, they were set alight. The intense heat generated by the roaring blaze struck us forcefully, even though we were ten yards distant from it. And both of us jumped up with alarm when, minutes later, the heads of the corpses exploded with two loud pops.

We were just preparing to leave when another angry young man turned up. 'You are tourists coming to see bodies burning, yes?' he attacked. 'But you are not understanding our religion. So why you come here?' I replied that these scenes gave us no morbid pleasure, but that we had simply come to pay our respects to the dead. Mollified, our guest insisted we take tea with his uncle. His 'uncle' turned out to be the proprietor of a silk factory. What a surprise. We were seated on a plush room-size cushion and invited to take off our shoes. Kevin surveyed my socks with distaste, and politely suggested I take them down to the ghats for ritual burning. Owing to mosquito invasions, they hadn't been off my feet for the last five days.

The proprietor, a fat, sleek individual, introduced himself to us as an 'honest businessman with genuine export connections'. After that, Kevin wanted to leave right away, but I persuaded him to stay. We were then shown some excellent samples of the 'factory's' wares, and were told that it specialised in Japanese cocoon silk – apparently the best there is – and that if we didn't believe this, we could test it by burning a few strands twisted between our fingers. This, the proprietor informed us, would supply an odour very much like the smell of burning flesh. However, since his shop lay downwind of the human funeral pyres and the sickly reek of burning flesh was all around us anyway, we really had no way of disputing his claims. In the end, on the slim off-chance that he was selling the genuine article, we bought a few samples and left.

Part Four

Basu and the Roof of the World

March 18ᵗʰ

After ten weeks in India, we left this morning for the Kingdom of Nepal. Kevin would be spending just seven days there, before returning to Bombay and thence back to England. For myself, I was allowing for at least three weeks in Nepal before getting back to grips with India once again.

We had booked the coach trip to Kathmandu via the Garden View Hotel. Included in the Rs550 cost was a 'free breakfast' at the Hotel Most Welcome near the bus-stand. It was here that we came across a young Canadian girl, Poonam, who had been born in India and who still spoke perfect Hindi. As we strolled up, she was just in the process of mopping a thick layer of grease off her 'free' omelette with a wad of toilet paper. Following her example, we listened on as she gave us many helpful hints. One thing she particularly warned us against was the giving of money to child beggars. It only encouraged them to leave school early, she said, and left them no option later on but to take up begging as a full-time occupation.

After eight long hours on the bus, we reached Sonauli on the India/Nepal border. We passed quickly through immigration, customs and police check-points, filling out forms all the way, and then took stock of our surroundings. Our first impressions were not good. The whole area round the border was derelict, filthy and generally unsavoury. And our 'free' lodg-

ings for the night – at the Nepal Guest House – were an absolute disaster. The food in its attached restaurant was under-
cooked, over-spiced (even by Indian standards) and totally inedible. Several of us got stomach problems there. A banana
pancake I ordered arrived with no bananas on it. Kevin ordered
a 'banana split', and that was precisely what he got – a lone
banana, with a split down the middle. Then Poonam turned up
weeping: she had just found two strange men sharing her
room. 'There is no problem,' claimed the manager, with an
arrogant grin. We suggested he put his sister or mother in a
room with two strange men, and wait for *them* to tell him what
the problem was. But he was intransigent. So we gave Poonam
our own room, and slept in the open dormitory instead. It was
full of restless, loudly snoring tourists.

Aggrieved by the manager's attitude, I strode off into the
dark for a quiet cup of tea. Before I knew it, I had wandered
back into India. The border had been empty – no security, no
police, no customs, nobody on duty at all.

Back at the lodge, a new friend – Trevor – recounted his
collection of Indian 'signs'. While some of the best had been
on buses (e.g. VIDEO IS NOT CONDITIONED and NO
STANDING ALLOWED), his favourite was a Bombay street
sign which had requested: PLEASE DO NOT COMMIT
URINE! I retired to bed in much better spirits.

March 19th

As we boarded the 8.15am bus to Kathmandu, the lodge
waiter came out to rant and rave at us for not paying the breakfast bill. If he called the evil slop he had served us 'breakfast',
we informed him, he was quite insane. I regretted having eaten

any of it. My stomach began to feel queasy.

And as the beaten-up, battle-scarred bus began to pick up more and more passengers en route, my seating space became uncomfortably cramped. Nausea began to sweep over me, along with a dawning realisation of ill-health. I was aware of Nepal's notorious reputation for sickness amongst travellers, but to be struck down on my very first day here – after such a good record throughout India – seemed so ridiculous that I determined to ignore it.

But I couldn't ignore it for long. Four hours into our journey, we made our only stop for food. Kevin and I opted for a sumptuous feast of dhal, plain rice and raw chipped potatoes. I stood up afterwards, and felt a strange, slimy, shifting sensation in my stomach. Moments later, the entire contents of my guts slid uncontrollably into my trousers. I just stood there, with a cup of tea in my hand, unable to believe what had just happened.

Watched by a couple of curious Nepali children, I dived round the side of the restaurant and abandoned my splattered underpants. Then I climbed back on the bus, and tried to convince myself that six further hours on the bumpy roof with chronic diarrhoea wouldn't be so bad.

Practically everybody on board had got on the roof of the bus by now. It afforded much better views. The route to Kathmandu took us up a series of narrow mountain passes, adjacent to which was a long, winding river. The only way to cross this rapid, powerful river was via the few frail rope bridges that had been thrown across. Ascending the passes, the bus skirted sheer-drop precipices at every turn and the grey-black foothills and mountains grew ever more formidable – until, at last, they blotted out the sun. With this, the wind blew icy and cold, and everybody on the roof stopped singing jolly songs and began to freeze to death. Prepared by the Patna-Nalanda run, I climbed into a sleeping bag and donned a thick sweater. Kevin was so desperate, he laid hold of a motorcycle helmet and strapped it round his head to keep his ears warm. The rest of him froze solid.

At one point (thankfully) the bus stopped for a flock of vagrant sheep, and I toppled gratefully off the roof, my trousers round my ankles, and helplessly squitted in a ditch. Looking up, I saw a whole bus-load of impassive Indian faces gazing at me with polite interest. I motioned 'Toilet paper?' at them, but none was forthcoming so I had to use dirty leaves from the roadside instead. I was so sick, I was beyond embarrassment.

We came into Kathmandu at 6.30pm, with grinning Nepalis clambering all over us and a sick woman liberally spraying vomit over every single passenger.

Off the bus, I wanted only two things – a room to go away and quietly die in, and a chemist to give me something to make it painless. A friendly tout tuned up to guide us to lodgings. But at the New Diamond Cottage, it soon became plain that he was a compulsive liar. Everything he'd told us about this place to get us here was a figment of his imagination. There were no single rooms, only doubles. There was no '24-hour hot shower service', only an overhead tap in the toilet with a thin, irregular dribble of cold water. And the hotel owner wasn't a Gurkha Buddhist at all, but a Brahmin Hindu. The owner apologised for our having been brought there under false pretences, and gave us a reduced room-charge. He told us that the touts who brought him business received 50 per cent of each placement, so that it was little wonder that they resorted to such incredible fibs to attract tourists.

I collapsed into bed at midnight. By now I was running a high fever. Only two things consoled me: it was refreshingly cool up here in the mountain valley, and there wasn't a mosquito in sight. Being ill in Kathmandu was going to be a breeze compared to India!

March 20ᵗʰ

Having left instructions for my burial with Kevin, it was a considerable surprise to wake up this morning. My limbs still felt like water, but I would survive. Giving way to a fit of optimism, I went down to the Central Immigration Office to arrange a trekking expedition into the foothills of the Himalayas. I figured this would give me an excellent reason for getting well again.

I obtained the standard seven-day trekking permit with ease. All they wanted was my passport, two photos, and proof that I had enough Nepalese money to survive up in the mountains should disaster strike. The whole thing took barely ten minutes. But if I thought this an improvement on Indian bureaucracy, I had yet to experience Kathmandu's Tourist Information Centre. This gave me no information at all. The centre was manned by a bored, resentful youth who deflected every question or request I made with practised ease. I came out no wiser about Kathmandu than when I went in.

Walking round, I began to draw my own conclusions. On the surface, the city appeared smart and clean. But the backstreets were absolutely filthy. Just off the spic-and-span main road, New Street, for instance, there was a butcher's shop with flyblown goat heads and bleeding cow legs on display in the window. Past the front of the shop flowed a gutter full of liquid faeces and offal. Another contrast was presented by the apparent respect for the smart, efficient-looking police and military force. I say 'apparent', because every Nepali we met in fact loathed the heavy presence of the military. They only put up with them because they defended the King, who is something of a major deity in Nepal.

The people of Kathmandu were a source of constant fascination. Even when they hassled for business or money, they did it with such charm and humour that you simply couldn't take offence. The children I saw were all happy, all laughing and all mucky and snot-nosed. They seemed particularly fond of running up and down the backstreets, guiding large wooden hoops along with small metal sticks. The Nepali men generally passed by in small groups, each of them smiling brightly and wearing their fez-like _topis._ As for the women, they were usually walking around with a large troop of tiny slant-eyed children in tow. These women were nearly all beautiful, and nearly all pregnant. They appeared a good deal more open and friendly than the women of India, and the relationship between the two sexes here in Nepal seemed altogether more free and natural.

Each of Nepal's three royal cities – Kathmandu, Patan and Bhaktapur – has its own Durbar Square, where all the main pagodas, temples and religious monuments are concentrated. The one in Kathmandu I found teeming with action and people – mainly Tibetans, Nepalis and Gurung mountain-folk in native dress trading in gems, knives, prayer-bells and others curios of tourist interest. There were also a number of tailors and clothes shops in this area, and a resident contingent of local musicians. Every one of them I listened to were performing 'Frere Jacques'. It was the only tune they knew.

This evening was a revelation. We came into Freak Street (so named because of its high population of hippies and spaced-out people) and found the Oasis Restaurant. Kevin went quite pop-eyed when he entered: all around him were display tables loaded with fresh apple pie, quiche Lorraine, banana cake and other culinary delights. After months of deprivation in India, it was almost more than he could bear. He gave a short grunt of disbelief, and ordered impossible helpings of everything in sight. By the end of the meal, we were both speechless. Kevin was in his seventh heaven. And I finished my repast with a 'Double Night-Life Special' (hot lemon laced with Khukri rum), which provided this excellent feast with the perfect complement. We retired to bed in the highest spirits for weeks.

March 21st

Travelling back to the Durbar Square by bicycle this morning, we met another of the friendly one-string fiddle players. This one wanted to sell us his fiddle. Kevin told him he had already bought a kerosene bicycle lamp (a most peculiar purchase) and that he had no money left. But the fiddle-player wasn't deterred. He began playing his instrument as thought his life depended on it. And he didn't just play 'Frere Jacques' either. He knew practically every Nepali folk-song going the rounds. A crowd of smiling locals gathered to listen to this charming performance with us. It was very good. But we still didn't buy the fiddle.

In Kathmandu, nearly every day is a festival of some sort. Today, the *Godejatra* (Festival of the Horse) was being celebrated. The streets were lined with laughing, mucky-faced children eating rice in leaf-plates, as between them passed a colourful performer twirling a long pole surmounted by top-knots of horse hair, as well as a small troupe of drum and flute players. We were just admiring this when Kevin spotted the Gurkha soldiers. They were passing by on parade. Kevin upped and bolted over to the sergeant, begging him for a photograph. To my great surprise, the sergeant brought the whole troupe to a halt, snapped them to attention, and let Kevin get his photo before marching them all off again.

What really made Kevin's day, however, was his purchase of an authentic Gurkha knife. And the manner in which he obtained it was quite extraordinary. One minute, he was sauntering indolently round the quiet Durbar Square, making casual enquiries about a souvenir pocket-knife to take back home. The next, he was surrounded by a bristling phalanx of traders, all urging him to buy the largest, most deadly blade possible. I couldn't believe my eyes. Looking across the square, with all those knives being whipped out and flourished in the glinting sun, it seemed to me that Kevin was on the point of being murdered. Rushing over to his assistance, I found him instead in ecstatic top form.

'Look what I've bought!' he exclaimed jubilantly. 'It's a knife!' I stared at it. It was more than just a knife. It was in fact the most scary-looking executioner's hatchet I had ever seen. Kevin told me it had cost him just £22, and began waving it experimentally in the air. Everybody instantly stood well back.

Back in our room, I was just having a quiet doze when I heard a strange sound in the background – something like a regular thok...thok...thok. What *was* Kevin up to? I opened one eye to find out. He was sitting on the edge of his bed, hunched up like a garden gnome, methodically chipping bits off his wooden washing-brush with his new knife. The brush stood end-up on the ground, and the brutal blade was whistling down on it in a flashing arc of moving death...only to stop short a moment before each impact and chip a tiny sliver of wood away, in preference to hacking a huge hole in the floor. 'What are you *doing?*' I asked Kevin. He looked up, surprised. 'I'm trying out my new knife, that's what I'm doing!' he retorted. And then he went back to work. By the time he was finished, the wood-block had been reduced to a neat little pile of wood shavings on the floor.

Later on, we went down to the Ratna Park to see the military horse-riding and acrobatic display, which was to be opened by the King of Nepal. But the King forgot to turn up, so the display never started. What an unfortunate lapse of memory on his part! The huge crowds outside the stadium turned increasingly ugly, and the police were forced to wade in and start cracking many heads with the long wooden stanchions called 'lathies'. It was a scene of total chaos.

March 22nd

As I popped the first 'beedi' (Indian cheroot) of the day into my mouth, I suggested that we celebrate my return to good health by spending the whole morning in the Oasis Restaurant. Kevin glanced briefly up from his resumed woodwork classes with the Gurkha knife, and smiled happily.

Kevin's 'breakfast' didn't finish until lunchtime. I let him go ahead, did my morning chanting, then wandered down to the Oasis. By the time I arrived he had already packed away a huge platter of omelettes, toasted sandwiches and banana cake. Then he decided to start all over again, just to keep me company. 'I couldn't possibly eat another thing!' he declared as I sat down, 'Now where's the menu?' By noon, Kevin was absolutely glutted. He sat opposite me holding his stomach, he eyes glazed right over and an idiot smile on his face.

The problem with Kathmandu, we decided today, is that it simply *eats* up money. We spent the whole day spending: on irresistible food (mainly cakes and confectionery), on attractive clothes and souvenir curios, and on entrance fees to temples. The very *worst* place we found for expense was Durbar Square. To linger here for an hour or so was to invite trouble, for a whole week's money disappeared before you knew it. Kevin accused me of trying the buy up the whole of Freak Street.

We also paid a quick visit to the unique Kumari Devi, an 18th century red-brick building full of exquisite wood-carvings, in which the famous Kumari ('living goddess') is housed. She is a young girl, always a virgin, who is hardly ever seen. She apparently only emerges from her secluded prison to bless prospective kings of Nepal, or to tour the city at the end of each monsoon. At puberty, the current Kumari is replaced by a younger one. The new Kumari is selected by placing ten small girls in a small locked room and frightening them to death for a whole night. The infant who is least paralysed by fear in the morning becomes the new Kumari.

March 23rd

Today was another festival in Kathmandu. This one was in honour of Hanuman, the Monkey God. The occasion was marked by twenty young men weaving drunkenly round Durbar Square carrying a huge effigy of Hanuman on a flower-decked chariot. Such was the weight of this thing that the carriers had no idea of where they were going. Before they had reached the end of the square, they had mown down one itinerant beggar, two stray flute-sellers, and finally a sleeping po-

165

liceman who lay across their path. Then, as the wild panoply of noise and colour reached its climax, one of the youths – a giggling, bug-eyed character – detached himself from the carriage and snatched up a duck from the roadside. The duck didn't know what hit it. One second it was strolling along the gutter minding its own business. The next, it was being hoisted up in the air by its feet and stuck under the processional chariot. As it squawked and flapped away in furious protest, everybody nearby clapped and cheered raucous appreciation. The duck was evidently a necessary addition to Hanuman's curious retinue.

Back in Freak Street an even stranger sight came into view – two young Nepal boys break-dancing on the pavements. Both wore leather jackets, tight trousers and dark sunglasses. They were both chewing gum and trying to look as ultra-cool and as much like Michael Jackson as possible. As time went on, we noticed more and more Michael Jackson clones wandering up and down the street. By the evening, we had learnt that Michael Jackson was, after the King of Nepal, the single most popular person in Kathmandu. The city was littered with Michael Jackson lookalikes, T-shirts, records, cassettes, stickers and badges; everyone here seemed to revere him as some sort of gum-chewing, highly fashionable Messiah.

March 24th

Getting up at 5am, Kevin and I walked down to the bus-rank by Bhimsen Towers, and bid our final farewells. Kevin dearly wanted to go on with me, but he was just about out of money. So his coach for Varanasi went in one direction, and my bus for Pokhara went in the other. For the last thirty days of my tour, I would be travelling alone. Or so I thought...

It was eight long hours later that the crowded, uncomfortable 'luxury' bus deposited me in Pokhara, at the foot of the Himalayan mountains. My backside was destroyed. A fellow passenger assured me that things could have been much worse, for had I taken the cheaper 'local' bus, I might well have arrived with no backside at all!

A wiry, grinning Nepali cycled up to me at Pokhara. He introduced himself as 'Juggernaut', and put me up in a private hut in the middle of a potato field for just eight rupees. Then he brought in a friend of his, Basu, who offered to be porter and guide for my forthcoming mountain trek. Basu was a clear-skinned young Nepali with a shock of black, greasy hair who smiled a lot. He agreed to take me up to Poon Hill, which affords one of the best views of the western Himalayan peaks, and then back again for a daily rate of NR40. We didn't discuss whether or not this rate included his meals and accommodation. This was a bad mistake.

Returning from the popular Baba's Restaurant, which looks over onto Pokhara Lake, my torch batteries suddenly gave out and I tripped over something in the dark road. It was a bookshop owner, who was lying here with his leg in plaster. He told me that he had broken it the day before in a glass factory. I asked him why he wasn't in bed, and he replied that his injury was good for business. 'If I am lying here like this,' he confided, 'people are feeling so sorry that they buy my books to make me happy!'

With no torch, finding my way back to the potato field in the pitch-dark was fraught with difficulty. It was not long before I stumbled knee-deep into a muddy quag at the side of the road, and resigned myself to the loss of yet another pair of precious socks. Another twenty minutes passed before, squelching my way miserably round the potato field, I happened on my small hut. I fell asleep, fully clothed and damp, as soon as my weary head hit the thin, dirty pillow.

March 25th

Having completed an excellent 'Big Breakfast' at Baba's, Basu and I hitched a lift into Pokhara Town from a passing Swedish resident in a jeep. Then, in view of our late start this morning, we opted to take a further jeep on to Suikhet instead of making the dry, dusty and dull five-hour trek there by foot.

This jeep ride was like taking part in a stock-car rally. The sturdy little vehicle charged relentlessly over pitted dirt-tracks, ploughed over rock-piles, plunged down into river gorges, and finally aqua-glided over rushing streams before depositing us, some two hours later, in the tiny trekking outpost of Suikhet.

On this journey I had two companions from Seattle, USA. Both of them sounded exactly like Henry Fonda. The three of us spent the bone-crunching trip with bandanas tied over our mouths and throats, to keep out the clouds of dust blowing regularly into the jeep. Basu, and the other Nepali passenger, looked at us mystified. They didn't seem to think this expedient necessary.

Basu's indifference to the dust had him coughing and blowing gouts of phlegm into his tracksuit sleeve the whole journey. As we alighted, shaken and breathless, from the jeep I realised that he had come down with a stinker of a cold. I asked him whether he wasn't better off back in bed, but he wouldn't hear of it. The ghost of a brave smile passed over his pale, fever-racked features, and he moved on ahead.

Tucked away at the foot of the mountains in a dry valley

bed, Suikhet town seethes with all the pioneering activity, and all the raw, rugged energy, of a Wild West trading post. Here, around the few rough eating-houses and lodges, local pilgrims, trekkers, mules, guides and porters laugh, and shout, and jostle each other cheerfully as they prepare to head up the mountain trails. The whole place is quite electric with the excitement of impending adventure.

From Suikhet (3,650ft above sea level), Basu and I set up the steep, rough-hewn stone stairway that marked the start of the trekking trail, and came one hour later to the lively little hill-village of Naudanda (4,675ft). It had been a hard first climb, and I took a glass of lemon tea to replenish lost perspiration. Naudanda's dry, dusty street was alive with goats, lambs and chickens, all running wild. By the roadside, local women – heedless of shame – bathed naked to the waist. Everywhere else, mucky, tousled children ran about, begging 'sweeties' from visiting trekkers and shyly picking their noses as they awaited a response.

I was just emptying my pockets of chewing gum for them when my meal arrived. It was a bowl of tepid, green curried water with two spinach leaves floating in it. The waiter called it 'vegetable soup'. I called it inedible slop. A faint sparkle appeared in Basu's moody, feverish eyes. His look dared me to eat this thin gruel, and to enjoy it. I let him eat it instead.

The warmth and companionship of the trekking trail soon enfolded me in its friendly embrace. All along the dry, dusty path, passing travellers shouted jolly greetings of 'Hello!' or 'Namaste!' – welcoming me into the camaraderie of the trekking circuit. I picked my way along the narrow trails, and soon noticed the long mule trains carrying heavy climbing equipment and trade goods up into the mountains. The 'lead' mules, wearing twice as many bells at the others (along with long feathered head-plumes), were instantly distinguishable.

Coming up towards Khare (5400ft), I began to take in the magnificent scenery. Way down in the valley below, Lake Phewa wound and glistened like a jewelled snake in the reflected light of the noonday sun. On the hillsides, women threshed wheat with powerful strokes of long cane sticks. Opposite, on the shaded mountain, slate-roofed Buddhist dwellings nestled in tiny rock clefts. Aged, wrinkled grandmothers walked up the track, bearing impossible burdens of firewood and fuel. An English-run 'nursery' for fresh fruit and vegetables appeared, set up on the edge of the slopes to catch optimum sunlight. And all around lay the massive black mountains themselves. Dark and forbidding, encircled by heavy mist, these sleeping giants awoke now and groaned in pain, as the warship prows of massed rain clouds clashed in wrath over their tranquil peaks, their wounded tears streaking downwards to bring, at long last, rain to the dry, cracked river-bed valleys below.

I had just left Lumle (5300ft) when the first drops of rain began to fall. And I welcomed the slight drizzle, for it tied the dust down to the trail and drove the close heat from the air. I came into Chandrakot soaked, yet refreshed. A look at the dark, lowering sky told me that a real storm was, however, not far away. Consequently, Basu and I agreed to remain the night in Chandrakot.

This was a small, quite primitive, village with just one or two lodges for travellers. Like most of the other buildings in town, the simple chalet we stayed in constructed mainly of wood, with some labs of mountain rock included, and the roof was neatly tiled with thin, resilient sheets of slate. Like most trek lodges, we were charged just Rs2 (five pence!) each for our tiny, bare dormitory cells, but were expected to eat all our food there.

I was becoming worried about Basu. He was getting more woebegone by the minute. As we sat down to supper, and as he studied me with hangdog hopeless dejection, I wondered again where his big smile had gone. I hadn't seen it since leaving Pokhara. To make matters worse, there was no electricity up here in the mountains, and a long, gloomy evening sitting in the dark, unable to read or to write, was an unbearable prospect. Soon, the sun's last rays faded over the storm-dark horizon, giving a last brief glimpse of the two ice-streaked giant peaks nearby. They reared up from the inky depths of the black hills like twin white whales, wreathed in a spray of ice-white mist.

I was saved from an evening of silent mourning with Basu by the unexpected arrival of two boisterous New Zealanders. They kept me entertained with stories of their travels late into the night. They were so entertaining indeed, that the lodge owner joined us, together with his three young sons. Everybody, including the children, were soon busily rolling up hash cigarettes and passing pipes of peace. A very mellow evening was had by all. Except poor Basu.

March 26th

Travelling up this damp, chill climate dressed in just a thin tracksuit, and armed with no sleeping bag, is not a sensible action for a mountain porter. Especially a porter with a bad cold. Consequently, Basu woke up this morning with double-pneumonia. It didn't seem to concern him at all. As he coughed and shivered his way downstairs to me, the only worry he had on his mind was his food and lodging bill. He wanted me to pay it.

This request came as a surprise. I had thought Basu responsible for his own expenses. Further, I had already spent nearly half the NR450 in local currency which I had brought on trek, most of it on buying Basu expensive fizzy drinks. When I explained my situation to him, he just shrugged and showed me his empty pockets. With a sigh, I paid his lodge expenses and told him to go home to bed. I wouldn't be needing his services anymore.

Proceeding on down the trek trail by myself, I took one look back. Basu was still standing where I had left him, staring after me. And his face hadn't changed. It still wore the same shocked look of surprise as when I had told him I was going on alone. He seemed to think I was crazy.

For the first few hours, I would have agreed with him. After almost getting trampled to death by donkeys and nearly falling off the cliff-face a couple of times, I began to realise how dependent I had become on following a guide's practised footsteps. With a heavy rucksack on my back, and little experience in negotiating the treacherous, crumbling rock paths, my trek suddenly transmuted from a jolly holiday into a gruelling forced march. It took me some time to realise the advantages of travelling alone – namely, that without a guide, one is not only saving money, but also able to rest where and when one likes, as well as meeting a lot more people. At first, however, all I could think about was survival. If you have an accident way out here, I had heard, the only way to get back home alive is to send out to Pokhara for a helicopter pick-up. I couldn't even afford a messenger, let alone the helicopter.

Having battled through the mule-trains, I came down the steep bath into Birethanti (3400ft). Then my heart stopped in my mouth. Way above me, my next objective, Hille (4800ft), towered a daunting two-hour climb up a sheer rock face. By the time I reached it, I was bathed in sweat and barely able to stand. Hille was a quiet place, a small Gurung-type native village with just a few empty cha-shops, wood shacks and traveller's lodges to its name. Coming into it, the dust-caked rock trail gave way to neatly layered stone paving. Packs of mules stood tethered in small corrals, resting after their hard climb. Elsewhere, a couple of ponies were rolling about in the dry dust. Red, white and blue flags fluttered on long bamboo poles, painted with prayer inscriptions. Hille was evidently a Buddhist village.

Feeling filthy but determined, I pushed on into the wild, rugged hinterland, beginning now to savour the pleasure of not having Basu around. Crossing over the charming rope-bridges at Tirkhedhunge (4900ft) indeed, I was actually enjoying myself. But then I looked up...and...up...and up, searching for the next point on my route. It was Ullere, a dizzying 2000 feet above me, at the top of a mountain. And the ascent was one sheer, unrelenting slog. It never levelled out at any point. Even passing pilgrims, on their way to Muktinath Temple, were having problems with it. Seasoned climbers all, they were without exception fagged out. A red-faced, sweating Australian chap passed me, going down. 'What a *sod!*' he puffed as he drew alongside. 'I tell ya, mate, I've climbed them all: Jomsom, Dhaulagiri, many other major peaks. But *this* bastard takes the biscuit!'

This climb finished me for the day. The views it provided, however, were spectacular. Rippling yellow harvest of corn and wheat stretched out below. Natural waterfalls gushed out of gashes in the mountain walls. Vast, yawning gullies dipped down into dry river beds. Meadows and fields shimmered gold and green in the glint of the sun. This was all very beautiful.

But nobody I met who had done this climb ever wanted to do it again.

I had been trekking some seven hours when I finally came into Ullere. I took a room at the Annapurna View Restaurant and collapsed on its veranda to die. Here I met the only other guest, a Dutchman called Joseph. He congratulated me on arriving just in time. 'Just in time for what?' I croaked. He pointed at the lowering sky and told me that a bad storm was coming. And he was right. Minutes later, the heavens gaped and the rain came down in sheets. Twenty-five other travellers crept into the lodge as evening approached. Every one of them was soaked to the skin.

The storm raged through the night. We sat under a canopy on the veranda to watch it. The black clouds crashed together like titans, sending claps of violent thunder rolling over the hills, and brilliant sheets of white lightning ripping open the dark canvas of the night sky. It was the most incredible natural firework display any of us had ever seen, and it sent the village dogs crazy. They howled their anguish right through the night.

I ate my evening meal of 'dal bhat', boiled eggs and curried vegetables in very mixed company this evening. Around the dim, candle-lit table were ranged travellers from France, from Switzerland and Germany, from Holland and Belgium. Few of us could speak each other's language, but all of us had by now discovered the lodge's unique 'outside toilet' and this provided a humorous conversation piece which transcended all national barriers. This outside loo was located in a small hut on the edge of a precipice, and the lodge owner wouldn't let you use it unless you promised to lock yourself in with a special key. Everybody thought this odd, but they understood his concern once inside. The loo was just two parallel blocks of wood laid either side of a big hole in the floor. You went in, squatted

down on the blocks, felt the gust of chill air wafting up your
nether regions, looked through your legs, and watched the bottom fall out of your world for a sheer drop of two thousand
feet! The reason for locking the door was obvious. Any unwit-
ting interloper who swung it inwards when you were squatting
over that hole was certain to knock you off your perch and
straight down it. And that would be a one-way trip to oblivion.
With your trousers round your ankles.

March 27th

Last night's rain had washed the mountains clear of mist, allowing a magnificent dawn view of Annapurna II   summit
from the lodge veranda. I watched this with Joseph, and with
two friendly young Germans, Peter and Thomas, before setting
off with them up to Gorephani Pass (9300ft).

This section of the trail was very attractive – full of red
rhododendron and white orchid trees, with much greenery.
Reaching the Pass some three hours later, I waited for the others to catch up and sat down to take a leisurely look at the rich
red blooms of the rhododendron forest surrounding me. The
sun was now high in the sky, sending sharp shafts of light
through the dark shroud of arboreal gloom and illuminating the
tranquil, sleeping woodland. Apart from the distant tinkle of
mule-train bells, all was quite silent.

Reaching the Riverside Lodge at the back of Gorephani
Pass, Joseph, Peter and Thomas became transfixed by its roaring hearth fire, and could not be persuaded any further onwards. Consequently, I climbed the final leg to Poon Hill
(10,500ft) alone, and took lodgings at the Hilltop Lodge near
the summit. This guaranteed me a good early view of the

mountains the following morning.

I was the Hilltop's last guest of the day. Moments after my arrival, a dense blanket of mountain mist swept over it, rendering it quite invisible to any further prospective customers. I was glad I had made the effort to reach this place – it also had a lovely, roaring log fire and I made friends with a young Canadian couple, Nick and Lorraine, who were 'collecting' memorable Indian signs. One of these, seen at Jodhpur rail stations, had a picture of man carrying a suitcase, followed by three small children blacked out by larger crosses. TRAVEL LIGHT! cautioned the sign. PLAN YOUR FAMILY! Elsewhere, Nick had come across a sign outside a Hindu temple instructing women having their periods to clear off. DO NOT ENTER WOMEN DURING MENSTRUATION! it cautioned.

As we all huddled over the warming fire, another fierce storm blew up. This one also raged through the night. Hailstones the size of eggs rained down on the thin tin roof of the lodge, making an incredible din. There was, however, one compensation. The storm, we knew, would certainly clear the mist for a perfect view in the morning.

March 28th

Everybody in the lodge was up early this morning, and trudging up the final twenty-minute ascent to Poon Hill's observation platform. Minutes after arriving here, came the dawn. The first rays of the rising sun pierced the horizon, striking the summits of Mt Dhaulagiri, then Annapurna I, then each of the lesser peaks in turn, illuminating their shaded peaks with an intense blaze of white light. Then the sun itself rose, a stately orange-red fireball, and the dark mask of shade over the landscape's visage was pulled aside, revealing thick forests of cherry-red rhododendron blossoms for as far as the eye could see below.

The whole range of western Himalayan peaks were now exposed, each of them shining forth with crystal clarity. As the eye travelled from right to left, Mt Macchapuchhre, then Annapurna I, then Nilgiri, and finally Dhaulagiri glistened ice-white against the dawn sky, with a whole vista of less prominent peaks interposed between them. All of us up on the observation point – our cares and worries and aching limbs forgotten – knew we were seeing one of the most beautiful sights in the world.

I returned to the lodge in excellent spirits, and took a good breakfast of porridge and honeyed Tibetan bread. Then I set off back towards Suikhet, on a return route that would take me an estimated three days. My estimate, however, began to suffer as soon as I ascended the black hills overlooking Gorephani Pass, and entered the notorious rhododendron forest blocking the route to Ghandrung. If you lose the trail here, say many travellers, you may never find it again. And I could well believe it. A short way into the thick forest, the trekking trail simply peters out and dies. More accurately, it splits off at regular intervals into a wide fork of false trails, most of which lead precisely nowhere.

My natural sense of direction being very poor, I was soon lost to the silent, smothering grip of the forest. A chill went through my heart, for I could see no way of getting out the other side. Then, at the point of total despair, I heard the sound of an axe in the distance, and traced it over to a lone woodsman who gave me a good set of directions. Without them, I might have been wandering that forest for hours, even days, making no progress whatsoever.

A single hour later, I broke out of the dense woodland and into open ground again. Now my only problem was the trail itself, reduced by the recent rain downfalls to a muddy, slippery death-trap. One false step on these quaggy slopes, and a broken leg or two was the very best I could hope for! But then, further up the track, I met Robert and Ismo. Robert was a swarthy, spade-bearded Italian giant, and Ismo, a small, pale elf from Finland. All three of us were having problems with the treacherous trails, so we decided to travel on together.

Descending greasy, hazardous slopes (with the constant risk of sliding down bottomless chasms), we were finally spat out by the black forest as the Purna Lodge, some four hours out of Gorephani Pass. A short rest here, and it was on through persistent rain drizzle via Bithanti towards Tadapani. I don't know how Ismo got round to tracking down Yetis at this point, but he did. As we ploughed through yet another boggy swamp of mud, dead leaves and dead rhododendron blossoms, he hopped forward – nose to the ground – following a series of curious three-toed footprints. It was only when we booked in for the night at the Mountain View Lodge in Tadapani, that he finally located his 'Yeti'. It was a Nepali porter, also staying at our lodge, who had been running on ahead of us all day. His left foot only had three toes.

As I hung my grimy, sweat-soaked clothes over the roaring lodge fire, I learnt from other travellers that I had been wise to take up with companions for this section of the trail, for it was apparently notorious for attacks by local bandits on people trekking alone.

The evening came to a lively end, with the lodge owner dragging in a big black goat from out of the rain, and then chasing all his chickens (hiding under our tables and chairs, near the warm fire) back into the cold again. The quiet lodge suddenly erupted into a squawking, flapping bedlam of flying feathers. None of the chickens wanted to go. One of them indeed was so against the idea that it flew into the flames and set fire to itself.

March 29th

I climbed off my bare-plank bed this morning cold and stiff. But I was beginning to enjoy the outdoor life up here in the mountains, and had decided to extend my trek. My seven-day permit expired today, yet there were so few check-points on the trails that I felt confident of not being challenged on the return to Suikhet.

By the time I arose, Robert and Ismo had set off ahead towards Ghandrung. After taking in marvellous views of Macchapuchhre and Annapurna South peaks from the lodge forecourt, I followed on. Today, the path had dried out and was good deal less muddy. It also ran relatively straight and even, allowing me to pay more attention to the surrounding fauna. Again, the dark forest, full of dangling creepers and red blossoms, claimed me, though now I was able to appreciate its tranquillity instead of being preoccupied with survival.

The thick woods suddenly parted midway between Tadapani and Ghandrung, and presented me with a scene of rare splendour. Far below lay the massive bowl of a dry riverbed valley, enclosed on one side by jutting hill-forests of pine trees and on the other by a raised cliff-plateau where Ghandrung village glittered bright in the sun. Behind was a backdrop of stout rust-brown mountains, over which the monstrous ice-streaked behemoth of Mt Macchapuchhre loomed, silent and grim.

The final walk down into Ghandrung was also a great pleasure. With the sun's warm, gentle rays playing on my neck and shoulders, I passed into the quiet rural hamlet alongside swaying fields of yellow corn and wheat. The air was musty and sweet with the odour of fresh manure and hay, and I came past the small thatched farmhouses waving back lazily to the local people and their children, filled with a sense of well-being.

I shared a bottle of Chang (beer) with a young Swiss couple at the popular Himalaya Lodge, and then plunged shakily some three thousand feet down into a deep gully via a very treacherous trail. At the bottom, I found Robert and Ismo waiting. They didn't seem very pleased to see me. My arrival meant they no longer had any excuse for not tackling the long, sheer climb up to Landrung. It was during this particularly arduous ascent that Robert fell and damaged his knee, and Ismo began to get heart tremors. We came into Landrung completely wiped out.

As he recovered, Robert saw an old local woman spinning wool on an antique Tibetan spinning wheel. He wanted that wheel. He wanted to take it home to Italy. I told him he'd be lucky to get it back to Suikhet – it weighed a ton. And the condition Robert was in, lugging a bulky spinning wheel twenty miles back across the trail would surely have been the end of him.

March 30th

Heading on towards Dhumle this morning, the level trail suddenly swept up into a steep hill-forest, forcing us to scramble up the sharp inclines on our hands and knees. Shortly before

Bhichuk, at the summit of this precipitous woodland, the silence of the forest was broken at last – by an army of giant crickets in the foliage, all chirping away in hypnotic harmony. Then it was up once more, a real grind, until we came to Pothana. Worn out, Robert grunted that this village name reminded him of a word – *putana* – by which Italians often swore, and that now he knew why.

We came into Dhumle (5900ft) after three hard hours climb, knowing that the worst was over, that now it was all the way downwards into the valley of Suikhet again. We rested on a lodge's green lawn, and peeled off our grimy, sweaty clothes to dry in the warm sun. Robert and Ismo promptly shifted upwind of me. They had just become aware of my socks. They were my very last pair, now set solid with grime and leaking an odious smell. I rinsed them out, and my companions cautiously rejoined me.

Returning down to Suikhet was not as easy as anticipated. On trek, one soon learns to look up and down and all around at the same time, but this descent was unprecedently steep and required our full concentration. Back on the dry riverbed valley, walking into Suikhet, we decided however to extend the trek one further day. All of us wished to head on up to the nearby point of Sarangot (5500ft) for a last look at the Himalayas before returning to Pokhara.

Consequently, at Suikhet we found a young Nepali guide who agreed to put us on the 'short cut' road to Sarangot, and to do it in just one hour (the usual route took three), since it was now already mid-afternoon. As we set off with him, I received a handsome offer of cash from a Japanese tourist who wished to buy my sleeping bag. I sold it happily. Not only was my pack now lighter, but the bag had not been washed in three months and badly needed fumigating.

The 'short cut' was a slog from start to finish. It involved a two thousand foot sheer ascent up a heavily-wooded mountainside, fighting the whole way through dense brambles, thickets and undergrowth. But we made it in one hour, as promised. Our loquacious guide reached the top scarcely winded. He had spent the whole climb talking Robert into parting with his sleeping bag. And he didn't rest until he had purchased it.

He left us at the crest of the hill, having put us on the right trail for Sarangot, and we walked along to the small village of Deorali Kaski. This was another occasion for great consumption of lemon tea, though we dared not dally long. We were slowly but surely being surrounded by a circle of local bandits, all of whom looked a good deal too interested in our bags for our liking. Again, I was glad I was not travelling alone.

Having left this danger-spot however, the rest of the walk into Sarangot was a real pleasure. Following in the footsteps of a local man – who paused from time to time to add to his arm-load of cow dung gathered from off the track – we came to a series of delightfully unspoilt farming villages. Here we passed many smiling, brightly-dressed women carrying large firewood loads, and were greeted with friendly waves from farm labourers returning from the fields. Children ran up to beg sweets and to hold our hands, and toothless old men – cackling merrily over musty old bottles of Raxi and Chang – beckoned us over to join them for a drink. Above, the sky echoed with the lazy caw of black crows and the sharp cries of fleet eaglets, and a light breeze sprang up, sweeping over the golden fields of corn and tugging stray wisps of straw from roadside haywains. Robert, something of a romantic, said it all made him think of a Van Gogh painting. He wished he'd brought his own easel and brushes.

We took simple lodgings at a small family house near the base of Sarangot Hill. The place was basic, but the occupants had real character. The landlord had a voluptuous young sister, who instantly took a shine to Robert. Watched by her expressionless kid brother (who resembled a diminutive bald Churchill), she sat Robert down and began stroking his stomach with a coquettish smirk on her face. It soon became apparent, however, that her interest was not so much in Robert but in his expensive cigarette lighter. The moment it slid back into his pocket, she slid out of Robert's lap and returned to the kitchen. Which was just as well, since otherwise we would have had no supper.

As the hearth-fire roared into life this evening, the lodge family joined us at our table, and bottles of beer and raw Raxi began to pass round. Not long after, the family discovered my cassette-recorder and began singing traditional Nepali folk songs into it. All of these songs were lively, lengthy and sounded exactly the same. I asked the landlord what they were about. 'Marriage song,' he replied. 'Which one?' I questioned him. '*All* are marriage song!' came the response. Then he led into another one. Soon everybody, including Ismo (temporarily forgetting his amoebic dysentery), was loudly clapping and banging kitchen utensils on the table in rhythm with the music. Following which, the whole Nepali family trooped out into the dark night and began dancing traditional jigs in the middle of the road. This went on till very late.

March 31st

This last morning on trek, we rose at 5.30am to catch the dawn. A short stroll took us up to Sarangot's observation point, a small bricked enclave flying a tattered Buddhist flag. From here, we had a perfect view in all directions.

As the fiery phoenix of the rising sun appeared over the orange-haze horizon, the entire eastern range of Himalayan peaks came into sight. And once more, as at Poon Hill (where we had viewed the western range), it was the summits of the highest mounts that first lit up with the dawn. Thus we saw Dhaulagiri first, followed by Annapurna and Macchapuchhre, and then the lesser peaks of Annapurnas III, IV and II. Down to our right, meanwhile, the wide, glittering expanse of Lake Phewa had become visible, the tiny veins of its many tributaries running into it from out of the distant mountain valleys. Directly below and forward of us lay the large, scattered complex of Pokhara Town, and down to our left plunged a deep ravine, leading down to a river valley of great beauty. It was a long hour before we left this magnificent viewpoint for breakfast.

The walk down to Pokhara lakeside was surprisingly intricate. We were all grateful that we had taken Sarangot from Suikhet, rather than (as is common) from Pokhara. The trail was difficult and poorly defined even coming down, so that many travellers seeking to reach Sarangot for its marvellous dawn views coming up were unlikely to reach it before noon. We passed at least a dozen ascending trekkers who didn't know where they were at all.

Back at the lakeside, we took cheap rooms at the Mahendra Lodge and stumbled off to the Hungry Eye Restaurant to celebrate our safe return with a rapid succession of cold drinks. The waiter simply couldn't serve them quick enough.

Over a delicious fruit muesli (chopped apples, bananas, oranges and papayas, packed onto a huge plate), I reflected on how much weight I had lost over the past week, and also on how much more healthy I now felt. Lots of good exercise, fresh air and simple food had done wonders for me.

My sense of fulfilment, however, was short-lived. Sitting still and doing nothing after a whole week of activity in the mountains came very difficult – to all three of us. By evening-time we were already fretting to be back on the trekking trail again. The rich, stodgy food, warm, muggy air, and lazy, laid-back atmosphere of Pokhara did not agree with us at all. We felt smothered.

April 1st

Over breakfast, I met Megan – one of four young Scottish girls who had spent the past six months working on a geological project (collecting fish specimens) in Nepal. We agreed to meet up again in Delhi, and perhaps do some travelling together.

As the day got under way, it became increasingly hot and sticky. After a regular diet of fresh, cool mountain air, we were floundering for breath until late in the evening. Only two activities helped us keep busy and distract our minds from the heat. Firstly, we took small canoes (kayaks) out onto the lake, the strong undercurrents forcing us to expend great energy to reach the small cove-beaches on the opposite shore. Second, we hired a bicycle between us, and took turns to explore our surroundings. I ended up snowballing down an incredibly steep hill, hurtling through a series of winding, cobbled back-streets, and sending a startled array of old men, children and cows flying, before jolting to a halt at the bottom. Robert had neglected to tell me that the bike had no brakes.

We should have liked to go swimming also, but Lake

Phewa isn't nicknamed 'hepatitis lake' for nothing. A bubbling scum of filth and disease covers the water in many sections, and few people take the risk of bathing in it. Most folk we observed were taking their minds off the oppressive heat by spending lots of money instead – either on rich food, or on Tibetan knick-knacks and curios, or on cool cotton clothing.

Travellers I spoke to today complained that the Pokhara Lakeside area was rapidly becoming over-commercialised, that every restaurant here now had taped music, home-cooked greasy apple pie, and a resident *sadhu* selling blessings outside. But, despite the heat and the mosquitoes, I began to notice one very good thing about it: namely, that it was the best place (apart from the trekking trail itself) for making new friends – or for hooking up again with old ones. Everywhere we went, travellers were flinging their arms around buddies they had met back up in the mountains, or somewhere in India, with the enthusiasm of long-lost relatives. No matter that both parties had often met just once before, over a dim, flickering log-fire perhaps. Here, as in India, acquaintances tend to be brief, yet really deep.

April 3rd

Back in the New Diamond Lodge in Kathmandu, I was woken up by a dawn chorus of howling hounds below my window. I hired out a bicycle, and travelled down to the Indian Embassy, intending to extend my visa for when I returned to India. Of all the embassies in Kathmandu, the Indian one is the most difficult to locate. And when I had found it, it was closed. The security guard at the gate told me that today was a public holiday. He couldn't remember which one.

A mop-headed little urchin raced up to me back in Durbar Square. He wanted to repair my shoes. Looking closer at him, I remembered that he was the same infant who had repaired my shoes the week before. I jogged his memory, and told him he could not have done a good job if the shoes needed repairing again seven days later. But he was sharp. He took one look at the mud traces on my soles and told me I had been trekking. I laughed and congratulated him on his deduction. He got his glue and sewing thread out and put the ragged trainers back together. An hour later, however, they had fallen apart once more. I tracked down the shoe boy and complained. He just shrugged and told me I needed a new pair of shoes.

The dogs outside my lodge appeared to have worn themselves out last night, for this evening all was quiet, and I finally got some much-needed sleep. Kathmandu, the second time around, was growing on me.

April 4th

The Oasis revealed a touch of class this morning, while I was eating breakfast, and began playing Vivaldi's Four Seasons on its sound system. One of my favourite classical pieces, it put me in just the right frame of mind to venture out by bicycle to the royal city of Patan.

Patan's attractive Durbar Square has just one western-style restaurant at present. It is called Cafe de Patan, and is owned by a beaming, broad-faced young man called Gun Muni Shakya (Gun) who runs his kitchen in between learning Japanese and break-dancing to Michael Jackson records. 'Gun' is a Nepali Buddhist, just nineteen years of age, whose father gave him this restaurant four years ago. In the course of our conversation, he told me of his eagerness to reach the age of 25, for then he would be married to a 'good Buddhist girl' and would not have to pay any further visits to the popular blue-movie cinema in town. He was rather puzzled when I explained to him the Western custom of fidelity after marriage. In his part of the world, because of severe restrictions on pre-marital sex, it was apparently common to take at least one mistress *after* marriage, which works out fine just so long as (in Gun's own words) 'wife does not find out of hanky-panky.'

The Durbar Square in Patan seemed somehow more 'authentic' than the one in Kathmandu. It was alive with people and chatter, markets and bazaars, atmosphere and colour. Within what was really quite a small square lay an incredible number of monuments, statues, pagodas and shrines. I sat back to observe them at leisure, and was particularly struck by the ornate dignity of the Garuda statue facing onto the magnificent three-storey Krishna Mandir. Then my attention wandered to the activity of the local livestock, much of which was roaming free in the busy square. Next to me, a sleeping man had acquired a curious companion – a large cow dozing on his feet. On the steps of the temples, meanwhile, scores of wild dogs could be seen fighting, playing or engaging in advanced sexual foreplay. Then a giant black goat appeared, strolling glassy-eyed down the road. It was promptly poked up the backside with a stick by some local adolescents, and ran amok. By the time it had quietened down again, a swathe of chaos had been cut through the marketplace – fruit, vegetables and indolent beggars having been sent flying into the air by the indignant goat.

I next took the bike to the Mahabouddha Temple or 'temple of a thousand Buddhas'. It was the place where my friend Gun had told me 'our god lives.' It was serene and quiet in the temple courtyard. Just as I got up to depart, however, the old guard sleeping under the shrine suddenly woke up and began ringing a loud bell. He then brought out a large fly-whisk and started waving it in the face of the red-faced Buddha in the shrine. A small child who had turned up to beg for a school-pen told me that 'now there are now flies on Buddha!

Having cycled back to Kathmandu, I dropped in on the cosy Mona Lisa Restaurant off Durbar Square for a lemon tea. This establishment had a charming sentiment on its menu:

We Serve to You and to your Guests with best possible Hot & Cold Drinks. We Honour our God when we Honour our Guest.

We serve Boiled and Filtered Water. Any complaints, Ask for That.

This evening, I teamed up with a dry-humoured Australian called Paul, and visited the renowned Yin-Yang Restaurant of Freak Street. The interior of this eating-house is a cross between a luxury penthouse suite and a film set for *Cleopatra*. The lights are low, soft music plays in the background, people recline and eat on soft silk cushions. The atmosphere is beguilingly relaxed and informal. Paul reckoned it was the nearest thing to 'divine decadence' he had come across in the East.

April 5th

I returned to the Indian Embassy again this morning, and arrived early, to be sure of being at the front of the expected large crowds for visa extensions. But the gates were closed as I cycled up. The guard told me that the embassy was closed again. Didn't I know it was Good Friday? I instantly gave up on the idea of getting my Indian visa extended, and decided to return to England a week early instead.

By contrast, the rest of the day went well. I took the bike out again, this time eight kilometres out of Kathmandu to Bodnath. This massive stupa, some 500 years old, is said to contain the relics of Kashyapa Buddha, one of the Gautama's predecessors. It is a large white-stone monument, covered with long streamers of coloured flags, and is painted with the yellow 'all-seeing eyes' of the Buddha.

The 40-minute ride to Bodnath took me through some charming little villages. Then, just before reaching the stupa, I dropped in on a small Buddhist prayer meeting taking place in a roadside shop frontage. People were just coming in off the street to squat down and support the ceremony. Within the small room, two facing rows of devotees methodically chanted off prayers from the high stack of small prayer-sheets before them. Their devotions were directed to the long table, at the back of the room, on which hundreds of tiny bells and candles stood, together with three decorated Buddha figures. Each prayer was punctuated by the blowing of loud matterhorns and the beating of strange drums resembling inverted frying pans.

Within the stupa courtyard, set back from the street, I talked to a Californian Buddhist whose Tibetan name was Tutod Dorge ('strength everlasting'). He was seated in the shade of the stupa's base, along with all the beggars and pilgrims taking alms here. Dorge was a rugged individualist, with weather-worn features and a pair of the brightest blue eyes imaginable. They twinkled, while he laughed. He laughed the whole time. He told me that all suffering was illusion, and that if people committed bad deeds against him, he just laughed at their ignorance until they apologised.

I sat down with Dorge and the beggars, and began to look at Nepalese life from the 'inside' for once. It was all very illu-

minating. Surrounded by gurus, holy men, cripples and destitute, I began to understand how they felt, and to share their
simple curiosity and amusement at the passing ranks of uneasy
American tourists being plagued by insistent peddlars. At one
point I stretched out my hand to say something, and one of
these tourists – thinking me a beggar – put a coin in it!

I was also struck, talking to these unfortunates, by their
wisdom, humour and undaunted courage. The crippled pilgrim
lying beside me, Siddhartha, had dragged himself all the way
up here from Delhi on withered legs no thicker than bamboo
canes, in his pure and simple determination pay respects to the
Lord Buddha. His closest companion – a nervous, dissolute
beggar called Ram – presented a complete contrast. He spent
the few alms he begged on the strong local Chang, and weaved
his way back to us progressively more inebriated as the afternoon wore on.

Amused by Ram's continual complaints that everyone got
alms but him, Dorge suggested he change his tack when begging. 'Stop chanting "Om-Mane-Padme-Om,"' he suggested,
'and try saying "Oh-money-give-me-some" instead!' This joke
really tickled all the beggars lining the walls of the stupa's
base. They were quite beside themselves with laughter. The
only person not amused was Ram. He had instantly tried the
new chant, but it didn't work.

Dorge took me along later to a small cha-house nearby, and
sent the grim, sour-faced housewife within into raptures by
giving her a string of precious prayer beads personally blessed
by the Dalai Lama. She was so overcome by this gift (the
Dalai Lama is considered a living god by many Nepali people)
that tears flowed freely down her face and she began to treat us
like royalty. Dorge commented that were one to travel up into
Tibet armed with a stack of photo of the Dalai Lama, one

could live like a king.

He then began to recount his life story. He told me that it was whilst fighting in the jungles of Vietnam, as part of the American forces, that he had suddenly 'seen the light' and decided to stop killing people. He had told this to his commanding officer, and had been sent straight away to a psychiatrist. It was decided that he was psychologically unfit to kill people anymore, and he was awarded a military pension on this basis. Since then (sixteen years ago), he had been travelling around with a developing interest in Tibetan Buddhism, which he liked for its sense of peace and happiness. He was presently on his way to a personal interview with the Dalai Lama, and would return to marry a Tibetan girl he knew, with whom he planned to set up a business in America, selling Tibetan carpets.

By the time we had finished our meal of vegetable *kothey* (small doughy dumplings like *momos*), I was however becoming concerned about Tutod Dorge. It wasn't so much his self-appointed mission as a spiritual teacher to mankind that worried me, but his apparently clear memory of past incarnations as eminent Tibetan lamas. Together with his belief in his probable descent from Jesus Christ himself.

I left presently, and returned to Kathmandu. Here, to my surprise, I met up again with Tim and Jill from Ooty, and took them to the Yin and Yang Restaurnat. After pointing out a gem on the menu – CARNAL CUSTARD – they entertained me with a list of Indian train signs they'd seen recently. Their favourite by far came from Londa Junction station, and it read: TRAINS RUNNING LATE MAY MAKE UP OR LOSE SOME TIME. They also told me of a strange contraceptive commercial they'd seen on Bombay TV. Its slogan read: USE 'NIRODH' FOR NEAR-NATURAL SATISFACTION AND

SPACING CHILDREN.

April 6th

Today I left Kathmandu again, for the ancient Buddhist stupa of Swayambu, which is some two thousand years old. Getting there involved towing my bicycle over a long and narrow rope bridge spanning the Vishnumarti River. Not only did the bridge have no hand supports, but there were several planks missing or collapsing underfoot, as well as a continual troop of heavily loaded villagers coming the other way. How I missed plummeting down into the boggy sewer of the river bed, I'll never know.

At Swayambu, I left the bicycle and climbed the steep 250-foot stairway up to the temple. There was an uncomfortable crush of tourists at the top when I arrived, so I went for a walk round the back of the complex until the crowd thinned out a bit. I came to a small courtyard housing a local Buddhist shrine, where all the local community were gathered together sharing a friendly 'holy day' celebration. I stayed here two hours, listening to impromptu performances of music played on drums, finger-cymbals, harmonicas and an ancient wheezing squeezebox. The local menfolk clapped along to the music, and took turns to 'guest' as singers with the small, lively band. Once more, anonymously melting into the background and allowing the rhythmic, hypnotic music to steal slowly over me, I was able to shed my tourist face and become just part of the local community. Somebody came up to tie a bright red string around my neck. All the guests at this cheerful little gathering, I noticed, had identifying orange cards tucked in their jackets or shawls. I don't think they were sure of my identity. The only other creatures present wearing the little red prayer-strings round their necks were a few local dogs and a couple of unlucky monkeys.

Back at Swayambu Temple, the crowds had at last gone and I was able to walk around in comfort. The resident animal community up here soon held my interest. A whole hierarchical society of wild dogs (around the stupa base) and wild monkeys (on the higher levels of the monument) had developed on this site. I took the opportunity to make a lengthy study of one of these canine 'families', living mainly on the leftovers being thrown out by the nearby *thali* restaurant. The mother bitch stood at rest, three large pups noisily sucking away on her swollen teats. Even when she moved off to forage in a filthy refuse bin, the tenacious triplets retained their hold, swinging off her paps like three determined little bulldogs.

In the meantime, the large orange mongrel who was 'Dad' sat guard and spent a lot of time sleeping. He only seemed to stir himself for two things: either to get the best of the pickings (generally banana leaves, with *dal bhat* remains clinging to them) thrown out by the food-house, or to interpose himself authoritatively between any other dogs who had disturbed his sleep by quarrelling. He was evidently the king of this patch.

At the base of the stupa steps, there was a 'fairground' for the local people in progress. It was a very small affair. There were just four stalls located on this clearing, the most popular of which was the hula-hoop stand. The 'big prize' here was a pack of twenty un-tipped cigarettes (price about 10 pence), so one could imagine how little money these poor people had to gamble with.

The major attraction, however, was the 'ferris wheel'. This was a light steel structure, groaning dangerously under the weight of twenty-four people, which was held together with just a few thin nuts and bolts. It was revolved slowly by two strong men and all the passengers, despite the imminent collapse of the fragile structure, looked absolutely thrilled. A young fairground roustabout (another Michael Jackson lookalike) came up to ask me if I wanted some heroin. When I said no, he suggested I might like a ride on the ferris wheel. I asked him what was more dangerous: the heroin or the ferris wheel?

Juddering my bike to a halt back down at the rope bridge again, I began to feel ill. The heat of the day was now at full intensity, and the awful reek of refuse, excrement and offal in the slimy riverbed below the bridge was quite nauseating. Crossing over with my bicycle was even more of an ordeal than on the way out. Then, just off the bridge, I looked up to see a tree whose branches were weighed down with a grisly burden indeed: a flock of giant vultures. I followed their steely gaze and saw, just to my right, a massive bullock being systematically slaughtered, skinned, gutted and chopped into small pieces. The butchers were surrounded by a crowd of clapping, appreciative infants. A refuse yard lay ahead; it was heaped high with skulls, bones and blood-streaked horns of various ex-bullocks. This ghastly pile of carrion was seething with flies and being picked at by red-eyed, scabrous wild dogs. And as I reeled down the street, overcome by the stifling odour of decay, filth and death, all I could see were wild pigs fornicating in the gutters, women and children urinating in public, and piles of refuse and flyblown excrement littering the dry-dust streets. I cycled out of this area as fast as possible.

I met up with Tim and Jill this evening, at the Palace Cinema in Naxal. Getting here was something of a problem, since at this time of day all the rickshaw drivers in town were set to shut up shop. Rather than say 'no' when I requested a ride to the Royal Palace (where the cinema was), they simply denied they knew were the Royal Palace was. Even when I insisted they *should* know, since it was principal feature of Kathmandu!

We had chosen to see the popular Hindi film *Sultan*, which Tim had been told would be easy for us to follow, since it had a lot of English dialogue. Unfortunately, it had no English dialogue at all, except for when the cast were in a bad temper and had to resort to foreign imprecations. The leading lady got really upset with the hero on one occasion. You could tell she was upset, because all she could think to call him (in English) was: 'You...you...*middle-class bore!*' The high spot of this film, however, needed no translation. It was a big musical number in which the whole cast ran about singing and spraying what appeared to be liquid blood all over each other with bicycle pumps. The number ended with everybody wallowing about in a mud-bath, singing at the tops of their voices, with nobody still recognisable as a human being. Other musical numbers had the obese hero trampling about on luxury sofas, wearing women's clothing, and the heroine running through the woods, trailing her laundry behind her.

April 7th

I arrived early at the bus-stand at Ratna Park, intent on visiting the third of Nepal's royal cities, Bhaktapur. From here, I would be making a one-day trek up to the heights of Nagarkot, which (on a clear day) is another fine viewing point for the Himalayas, and particularly for Mount Everest.

The bus to Bhaktapur was like travelling below deck on a slave ship. The tiny minibus was only designed to seat twenty people, with room for another seven standing. How *fifty-six* passengers managed to cram into it defied the laws of physics. I sat outside the vehicle and watched everybody scrum frantically into it, and drank a cool Limca while they all simmered away inside for the next twenty minutes. The close heat within the stationary bus was formidable. When it finally made to leave, I leapt up and jammed myself in the back. Twenty minutes later, I crawled off at Bhaktapur bent double and with my left arm twisted behind my head.

Bhaktapur, being the least accessible royal city of Nepal, is also the most unspoilt. Its quiet and stately Durbar Square was a good deal cleaner and less populated than that of Patan or Kathmandu. Walking down a small side-street, I came to its magnificent five-storied Nyatopola Temple, which was situated in a small, lively market square all of its own. Taking lunch at a small pagoda-style restaurant here (which had a priceless toilet sign: PLEASE PUT UNDISPOSABLE DIRTY STUFFS IN THE BIN), I observed the two huge processional 'juggernauts' used to carry the temple gods round town at festivals, and gradually talked myself round to commencing the trek up to Nagarkot.

The climb up to these heights is a complicated one. On a good day, one can expect to make it in four hours. On a bad day, with all sorts of false trails cropping up along the route, you don't make it at all. This felt like a bad day. The heat was overpowering, the air was enervatingly close, and my innate poor sense of direction concerned me. I studied the map again and again, and then decided to trust in whatever gods were looking after me and set off up the road.

I needn't have worried. The local people of Bhaktapur gave me perfect directions for getting out of the city, and I reached my first landmark, the Army Barracks, with no problem. Feeling optimistic, I decided to attempt a series of short cuts across country, rather than taking the dull route up the winding main road. To my relief, just as I struck off into the great unknown, a young Nepali boy turned up. He knew the shortest routes possible to Nagarkot. Carrying two boxes of shoes he'd just bought in Bhaktapur, and whistling for all he was worth, he led me a fierce military pace down a quiet, lonely trail which ran parallel to the city's water pipe, and which led into beautiful country and farmland scenery. We passed down winding lanes, through a gauntlet of blooming red-rose bushes full of tiny, twittering birds with white-tipped wings. Then we came over a small rickety wooden bridge, below which ran a babbling brook, and soon reached the end of the valley. Here there was a large dam and my young guide took me off the level plain and up a sheer hillside, through thick forests of pine trees. Breathlessly emerging at the top, I found that we had reconnected with the main road again, having shaved a whole hour off my scheduled arrival at this point. A short way up the road, my diminutive helper came to his house and bid me farewell. His house was right next door to an ancient Buddhist stupa.

A few minutes later, just as walking on asphalt was becoming tedious, another young lad popped up to show me another short cut route. He pointed to a high stile on the side of the road, and told me that if I crossed it I should save myself another half-hour on my journey. He was right. I reach the foot of Nagarkot having walked a total of just two and a half hours. Which was much better than four hours, and a good deal better than not getting there at all!

Near the summit, yet another mysterious helper appeared to direct me to a good lodge. This was the Sunray, on the crest of the mountain viewpoint. The dormitory room I booked at this pleasant hostel had just one other occupant – a quiet, dry-humoured Australian girl called Jenny. She was also travelling solo. Over our dal bhat supper, seated round a bare table lit by a single flickering candle, we exchanged experiences of India and admonished the acquisitive Nepali landlord for funding his regular flights to London and Melbourne by charging prohibitive food prices to poor tourists like ourselves. He gave us a simple choice: pay up or shut up. But he did it with a smile.

April 8th

Rising at 5am, we crossed up to the top of Nagarkot ridge expecting a glorious view of the Himalayan peaks, including Everest. But it didn't happen. The heavy heat-haze rising from the plains below still hung like a shroud over the horizon. Last night's light rainfall had been insufficient to disperse it. There was, however, one compensation: an awesomely beautiful sunrise. As Jenny and I peered into the lightening gloom, the sun emerged like a ghostly red will o' the wisp from the dank marsh of fog lying over the mountains. Its dim lantern-light illuminated them for a brief space, and then the clouds rolled back again and all was lost to view. For these few minutes, however, the sight had been one of rare beauty.

The small minibus returning to Bhaktapur at 8am had twenty-seven people on the roof. We knew that, because Jenny and I were up there too, and we counted them. It scarcely seemed possible. And it certainly wasn't safe. But the journey proceeded without incident, and the view on the way down – overlooking picture-book hamlets, villages and countryside – helped us forget our discomfort. Back in Bahaktapur, the cool, clean mountain air was instantly replaced by the cloying heat, dust and smells of humanity and decay. We took a brief look at the town's famous 'Peacock Window' (one of the finest wood carvings in all Nepal) and then immediately set back to Kathmandu. The heat was overpowering, and both of us needed a nice cool shower.

I was, however, to be disappointed. Arriving back at the New Diamond Lodge – tired, hot and sticky – I learnt that my shower was 'not possible', because 'water is off.' Displeased, I demanded to know when it would be 'on' again. I informed them that I had now spent a total of six days in this lodge, and had not yet managed a single shower. The manager, yet another young Michael Jackson clone, was not used to being admonished. He just stared into his lap, looking sulky and bored.

April 9th

I don't know why I decided to return to Delhi by bus. Long, uncomfortable bus journeys in India should have convinced me by now that Asian buses and I just didn't get on. But for some reason – probably because I was now so keen to return to Delhi for my post, and because this was the quickest way of getting there – I managed to book myself onto a gruelling 36-hour bus trip from Kathmandu to New Delhi. It was sheer folly.

To its credit, the vehicle standing in Kathmandu bus-station this cool morning was the nearest thing to a 'luxury' bus I had seen in the East. It had padded seats, sufficient leg-room and windows that didn't rattle. Further, I had supportive English fellow-passenger in front and behind who kept me in food and cups of tea when (very shortly) my Nepalese money ran out. All looked set for a calm, pleasant journey.

We left Kathmandu at 7.30am. It was still refreshingly cool.

A couple of hours later, it was quite a different story. Descending from the high valley into the hot, blasted plains below, the atmosphere became uncomfortably muggy and close. Soon all aboard were wheezing and gasping for air out of the windows. By noon, the interior of the bus was like an oven. My nose, throat and mouth were dry as sandpaper, and I began to feel feverish with the heat. A raging headache seized me, and my brain felt like it was cooking inside my skull. I was reminded of one of those unfortunate funeral-pyre corpses at Varanasi, sizzling away to a charred heap of melted remains.

But it was when we reached Sonauli again, at 4.30pm, that my troubles really started. At the border, customs officials boarded the bus and began searching passengers. This search took three long hours, and all this time we were confined to our seats, baking to a crisp in a bus that had reached the temperature of an overheated sauna. The cause of the customs officers' extended interest was a grinning Nepali they had found wearing a bright-blue tracksuit. They had gravitated to him immediately. Nobody in their right senses would wear a thick woollen tracksuit in this heat. He evidently had something hide. And yes, he *did* have something to hide. Under his bright-blue tracksuit, he was wearing five more bright-blue tracksuits. And twelve pairs of luxury underpants. And seven pairs of socks. And a dozen silk handkerchiefs. One wondered how he had survived wearing this little lot, when all the rest of us were passing out in the pre-storm heat dressed in light cottons. The customs men didn't seem surprised, though. They grinned at the overdressed smuggler, and he grinned back, as though this was the most natural occurrence in the world. Still grinning, the customs officials proceeded to go up on the roof and sift through all his bags and belongings. Searching for more contraband. One of them stayed below, and occupied himself by interrogating two harmless Buddhist monks seated within – looking in between the seams of their sandals for flattened strips of hashish. After two hours of this, the Nepali got fed up of grinning away in the sweltering heat, dressed in all his tracksuits, and summoned the customs men down from the roof. He grinned at them, and they grinned at him, and then he gave them the 'baksheesh' they had been waiting for all along. We were free to cross the border.

On the other side, I fell off the bus – steaming like a radiator – and downed a whole pot of tea. Then I staggered back, climbed up onto the roof, and lay there panting like an old man. The bus driver began jumping up and down in wrath below, ordering me to get back inside. I told him not likely, and would he care to send up a wreath, since I didn't expect to reach Delhi alive. Three other dying people crept up onto the roof, and lay down beside me. The bus roared off into the night, and we closed our eyes and wondered if and when this nightmare would ever come to an end.

Finally, the storm broke. The sky crackled, the thunder rolled, and the rain came down in a solid sheet. On the roof, our cracked and dry mouths opened to receive the moisture, and we gave a concerted feeble cheer. Best of all, a strong breeze had blown up and this, together with the rain, soon drove the smothering mugginess from the air, leaving it fit to breathe again. We returned back to our seats within the bus, sure that now the worst was over.

But it wasn't. In the middle of what was to be a long, long night, I came down with chronic diarrhoea again. It came very suddenly, and it struck very hard. Every stop we made, I would be clambering over sleeping bodies and vaulting out of the bus into dark trenches and ditches, moaning in agony as yet again the bottom fell out of my world.

This went on right through the night. But at least I wasn't alone this time. After a while, the quiet, friendly German chap sitting next to me also got struck down. Every toilet-dash I made after that, he would be padding companionably along behind me. It felt a lot less lonely, the two of us groaning away together in the dark roadside ditches. Fortunately he was the only person on the bus who had a toilet roll to share.

Even so, the ordeal was a miserable one. My idea of the ultimate purgatory was no longer forty-one hours in the coffin of the 'Express' train from Delhi to Madras. For sheer sustained awfulness, thirty-six hours in the jolting, heaving oven of the Kathmandu to Delhi bus – travelling through drought, tempests and customs points with no food, no water, no money, no toilet roll and chronic dysentery – really took some beating. Able to sleep only in fits and starts, I spent the rest of the night in a trance of dejection, composing imaginary epitaphs for myself.

Halfway to Delhi, the bus hit a gigantic pothole in the road and leapt into the air. When it came down again, it did so with such force that I was catapulted out of my seat and had my nose smashed into the luggage rack above my head. All in all, I thought, this had been just about the worst day of my life. But then, I didn't know about the day to come.

April 10th

Things went from bad to worse. Purgatory no longer sufficed to describe what I was going through. This was Hell, and nothing less. Other passengers suggested I eat lots of curd at each stop, for this would set like concrete and steady my stomach. But it didn't work...It went on and on, until I simply abandoned myself to my fate. By now I felt like I had made the acquaintance of every roadside ditch and slit-trench in India. The attacks were soon coming so fierce and fast that I couldn't even get to a ditch, but simply fell off the bus with my trousers down, ready to go where and when I dropped.

But all good things must come to an end. The bus rolled into Delhi at last, and I managed to keep my trousers up long enough to stumble off with a semblance of dignity. My mind, body and spirit were however in a state of complete turmoil. The last few hours of that journey had been the worst kind of medieval torture. I simply couldn't believe it was over. It was like being plucked, only mildly protesting, from a living grave.

I caught a rickshaw back to the Hotel Chanakya, and asked for a room with an attached toilet. They didn't have one. They offered me a room with an outside toilet instead. I told them to forget about the room, and to just rent me the outside toilet. They didn't seem to think I was serious.

It was 9pm when I arrived at the Chanakya. It was a long hour later that I finally emerged from the outside toilet. There was a long line of Indians standing outside with toothbrushes, looking impatient. I told them to complain to the manager, and crawled over the road to find a chemist. The chemist listened to the account of my illness with increasing alarm, and prescribed me his strongest medicine. It didn't work.

Five more attacks during the night left me totally destroyed. And convinced me that the Kathmandu to Delhi bus was fit only for lemmings or for people seeking a really painful way to die. If I ever did it again (and this would only be under extreme compulsion) I would take a rucksack full of toilet paper and would take care to write out my will first.

April 11th

I moved all my essential belongings over to the outside toilet this morning, and barricaded myself in. A storm of angry protests from hotel staff and guests failed to dislodge me. Through the toilet door, I gave the Chanakya manager a non-negotiable ultimatum – either he gave me a room with a loo in it, or I would stay where I was. In my condition, I was prepared to stay there all day if necessary. The manager gave in, and promised me a new room.

The new room had a loo in it. It didn't however have any windows. Small, dark and enclosed, it reminded me of that awful, claustrophobic bus. I skulked around in here for a while, then felt the walls closing in and went up to the manger and demanded yet another room. He sighed patiently and gave me the last room he had. This had windows in it, and a loo. It also had a team of workmen hacking bits of wood about right outside my door. My nerves on edge I went back in search of the manger. But he had fled, and left a deaf receptionist to deal with me instead. This fellow was so absorbed in his paperwork that he didn't even look up when I lodged my complaint. So I took away the paperwork, and repeated it. His sharp beak of a nose finally crept off the desk, and he surveyed me with puzzlement. He didn't look like he'd ever received a complaint before. He didn't know what to make of it. Finally, he told me that the offending workmen would be finished soon, and would be out of my way. They were just making a new toilet door.

Passing down Main Bazar Road, I found far more suitable lodgings at the Queen's Hotel. Not only was it cheap (Rs35), but I had a loo, windows, two beds, a balcony leading onto the roof, and no workmen making noise outside. It was a real find.

Today, in the park opposite the Poste Restante, I saw a bullock mowing the lawn. It was hitched up to a rotary mower, and ambled erratically over the grass under the indifferent supervision of two half-naked herdsmen. Both had little cane whips, which they listlessly flicked over the bullock from time to time, probably to keep the flies out of its eyes.

A short time later, returning to my hotel by rickshaw, I passed a giant spade-bearded Sikh standing on the kerb. He wore a manic grin and his wild eyes gleamed with ferocious joy. He seemed to be some sort of popular magician. A large, curious crowd had gathered to watch him give a dazzling display of flashing sabres at the very edge of the passing traffic. Nearby, I saw a cycle-rickshaw rider sitting in the gutter rubbing his head. It was bleeding. The look he was casting at the performing Sikh suggested that he had just driven too close to the flashing blades and had had his hair parted for his carelessness!

April 12th

My chanting seemed to have a pleasant, soporific effect on the Indians staying in my lodge. They all assembled companionably on the roof to listen in as I began my prayers, then drifted over to go to sleep or recite Indian sutras to each other under my window. I was most touched.

I visited the Plaza cinema this morning, to see a Hindi comedy called *Jewel Thief*. It was really rather good. In fact, it was so good that I managed (for the first time with an Indian film) to sit the whole way through it. Even when it ran over three hours, and even though I had not yet had breakfast. My interest was held by the male lead, who was a dead ringer (though a few shades darker) for Cary Grant.

The plot of this picture, like so many Indian movies, moved at a very rapid pace. So did Cary Grant. He was continually running away from grossly overweight Indian ladies trumpeting love songs at him. He hardly had any time to be a jewel thief. And he was so tired from side-stepping buxom songstresses that when he managed to land a weary punch on some villain, his heavy heroine had to scrape him off the pavement and drive him home to recover.

The golden rule in Indian films of this sort is that the woman who sings best (and loudest) gets the hero. It doesn't matter if other women have the faces of angels or the figures of Titian goddesses. If they can't sing, they don't get a look-in. The hero won't even acknowledge their interest. In this film, the heroine (i.e. the woman who sang best) resembled a gargantuan, doom-laden Cassandra. The only time she wasn't prophesying disaster or feeling certain of impending tragedy was when she was singing. Which was a pity for 'Cary', because he would have been far better suited to the nubile, petite secretary who kept trying to drag him off to bed. The only trouble with her was that she couldn't sing. So he had to pretend to be bored every time he saw her. The man was so perfectly under control, that he could appear bored and indifferent even when surrounded by the state guard, a posse of trained snipes and three elephantine women who couldn't sing. The only time he didn't look cool was when the script required him to sing a love song on a mountain top dressed in lederhosen, a little red waistcoat, a limp brown tweed jacket, a huge bearskin hat and a pair of brilliant-black pointy shoes. Nobody could look unconcerned in that outfit.

The film came to an end very suddenly. There was no warning, no fade-out, no credits, no closing curtains, nothing. Just a bare, empty screen.

April 13th

As I lit up the first Panama cigarette of the day, I reflected that the more I saw of India, the more I liked it. Wandering through the streets, and observing the many herds of sacred cows, for instance, I could now view them as amiable, benevolent spirits rather than unnecessary public nuisances. Previously, I had been irked to hear that there were twice as many cows in Indian than human beings, and that this explained a lot of the prevailing food shortage. Now, however, I could see some of their value. Not only did their endless patience and calm stoicism impart some sense of order and tranquillity to busy Indian streets, but they also managed to keep the accumulations of waste and rubbish on the road down by eating a remarkable amount of it.

Part of my misconception of India, I was now coming to realise, lay in the fact that foreign tourists like me only saw a certain 'type' of Indian – generally the type who wanted money. The vast majority of Indian people are of course neither insensitive nor grasping.

I had further evidence of this when I joined a cinema queue for an English film this morning. It was a very long queue, and I was standing at the back of it with minimal expectancy of getting a ticket. Suddenly, a smiling Indian youth came up to me and said: "Do you want ticket?" Fully expecting him to be a tout, I snapped back: "And how much is *that* going to cost me?' But I had misread the situation completely. He wanted to *give* me a ticket, not sell me one. As he went away, offended, the 'house full' sign went up and I realised that I would now never get in. Going over to the helpful Indian, I apologised for my misunderstanding and he laughed and said he quite understood. Walking on, however, I determined from hereon to always listen to people who came up to me, before passing adverse judgement.

It was while buying some cakes in Wengers, in Connaught Place, that I met up again with Megan, the Scottish girl from Pokhara. Over a delicious iced milk-shake, we exchanged tales of our separate travels, and I invited her to join me next week in Rajasthan.

Further along Connaught Place, we went into McDowell's Pizza King for lunch. This establishment was celebrating some sort of anniversary. To mark the occasion, it had two guitarists singing woeful renditions of old favourites by Simon and Garfunkel. There was a curious card on our table. It said TRY ONE OF OUR CHICKEN AND EGG RELATIONSHIPS.

Part Five

Revelations in Rajasthan

Many western travellers go to Rajasthan for a rest at some point. One of the quietest states in India, with a relatively low population, it is also one of the friendliest and most attractive. Having now journeyed the length and breadth of this country, I decided the time had finally come to give myself a 'holiday' before returning to England.

Teaming up for this excursion with Jenny – who had turned up from Nepal yesterday – I boarded the noon train to Udaipur and joined her in the ladies' compartment. It was nice and quiet in there – we were the only two occupants.

Things went well until, at 6pm, we came to Rajgarh (just up the line from Jaipur) and then our luck ran out. Firstly, the train developed a fault and stayed put in the station, awaiting repairs. Then our compartment was suddenly invaded by a large family. The parents were quiet enough, but their three boisterous children created havoc. They leapt and cavorted all over the seats, shrieking loudly the whole time. Meanwhile, the parents – making no attempt to curb their wild spirits – just smiled at them indulgently, apparently condoning their attempts to demolish the carriage. There was also a fourth child, a small baby, present. It lay in a small bundle on a seat, sound asleep through all the bedlam. The other children, not liking this non-participation at all, decided to wake it up. One of them began playfully head-butting it on the seat, while the other two shoved entire orange segments into its tiny buttonhole mouth. It wasn't long before it too started screaming, providing a perfect backdrop to the resumed cacophony of its elder siblings.

I beat a tactical retreat at this point, leaving the stationary train for a brief foray into Rajgarh village. Poor Jenny, suffering from the heat and the children in the compartment, croaked relief as I returned to hand a bag of apples and mandarin oranges through the window. She informed me that we had now been delayed over two hours.

Shortly after the train set off again, at 8.30pm, I was shunted along by the guard to my correct sleeping berth, four carriages down from the ladies' compartment. I found my 'reserved' bunk full of other passengers' luggage. And they were most reluctant to move it. Only when I indicated that I was likely to be sick all over them unless I was allowed to lie down, did they finally relent and clear the bunk for me.

The lights in the compartment went out. The Indian below began snoring, but that was okay. I was used to that. Everything else was pleasantly quiet, and I prepared to get a good night's sleep. Suddenly, however, another man arrived and rudely shook the snoring Indian awake. He wanted to talk to him. A loud, spirited conversation sprang up beneath my weary head. I took about ten minutes of this and then, realising that it was likely to go on all night, I told them to put a sock in it. The 'visiting' Indian looked up at me in astonishment. He evidently did not think that holding a loud conversation in a compartment full of sleeping people at midnight constituted any sort of nuisance. But he took the hint, and left.

A few minutes later, I heard an odd hissing noise below, and leant over the bunk to investigate. He was back. My nocturnal nemesis was now kneeling below his companion's bunk, resuming his conversation with him by means of agitated *whispers*. Oh well, at least I'd tried. I put my earplugs in, and eventually drifted off to sleep.

April 15th

Arriving in Udaipur, we took a cab down the quiet, dusty streets, and booked into the Rang Niwas Palace Hotel, which in better days accommodated the Maharani of Udaipur's guests. Over a century old, it was still however a marvellous building – set in green gardens full of exotic birds, sculpted bushes and orange-blossomed acacia trees. As we moved in, the lodge's cocker spaniel was wearing itself out barking at a vagrant cow that had wandered in from the street. Then the cow left and all was quiet.

After a refreshing shower, we walked along to Udaipur's magnificent City Palace. The views from its turrets and balconies were quite breathtaking, particularly those of the famous Lake Palace below and of the desert mountain range in the far distance. The palace itself was a marvel – jewelled mirrors, ornate mosaics, intricate latticework windows and colourful peacock sculptures. These treasures combined with rich silverwork, beautiful tapestries and awesomely decorated courtyards, to produce a magical effect of opulence and extravagance.

Walking down to Pichola Lake, we then took the popular speedboat ride across to the fabulous Lake Palace, situated in the middle of the landlocked waters. The place, now turned into a hotel for rich tourists (Rs300 per night for a room), had plush carpets, antique t'anka tapestries on the walls, and grandiose chandeliers and brass lamps dripping from the ceilings. Jenny and I rested in the 'Coffee Room', watching as flocks of sparrows swept back and forth over our heads and breathing in the sweet smell of honeysuckle emanating from the nearby tea garden. Soon, as the sun set over the metallic-red lake, we took our leave and returned back to land.

We dined this evening at the nearby Roof Garden Cafe, an excellent viewpoint from which to observe the twin royal palaces. At night, both palaces are beautifully illuminated and stand forth like a pair of gem-studded, glittering crowns on the regal brow of the hill opposite.

While we were looking at the Roof Garden's menu – which offered COD COFFEE and FRUIT SALAD WITH RESINS – a sleek, refined Indian sat down at our table. 'Call me God,' he announced, translating his Hindi name, Dev, into English for us. He had seen my Walkman cassette recorder and was interested in buying it. He remembered seeing us in the Lake Palace hotel earlier, for this was where he worked, managing the coffee bar. Aged just 26, Dev was very affluent by Indian standards, managing to support a large family in a big house with three flats, and able to fully indulge his two favourite hobbies – riding powerful motorbikes, and drinking large rum and cokes. All he needed now, he reflected while smoothing his neat pencil moustache, was a rich wife. The rest of the evening he spent staring at Jenny. She looked eminently suitable.

April 16th

Udaipur at this time of year is incredibly hot. The sun beams down like a laser, and animals and humans alike retreat gasping into the shade, and go to sleep. Somehow, Jenny and I roused ourselves to activity. Hiring bicycles, we undertook a sightseeing tour of the city.

Cycling was surprisingly cool. We creaked happily through a number of identical sleeping streets, and arrived at Udaipur's famous puppet exhibition, the Lok Kala Mandal. Here we were the only guests. The yawning attendant told us to sit on a carpet and wait for the puppet exhibition. Twenty minutes later, nothing had happened and we rose and left. On the way out, Jenny pointed out a wall photograph of a young native girl in full tribal regalia. The inscription read:

The Adivasi Belle from Gujarat is child-like in her ways. She combines a jazzy blouse with heavy bangling necklaces and intricate bracelets. What does she care for aesthetics? She is a child of the soil!

Behind the gardens of Sahelion ki Bari, we later came across Udaipur's 'Science Museum'. The most recent scientific advance depicted here was model showing how electricity was invented. Elsewhere, there was a collection of the most bizarre exhibits – some old skulls in a corner, a damaged stuffed bat (with a fox's head) hanging off the wall, and a vast number of small animals and reptiles crammed into pint-size milk bottles. Then we came two large glass cages. The first contained a life-size model of a naked women, with detachable breasts and a detachable face. Behind the face lurked some sort of green cancerous fungi sprouting all over the surface of the brain. In the second case stood a skeleton wearing a green and white sari. It had a broken arm, which hung limply at its side, and its lifeless skull gave us a macabre, empty grin. We concluded that it was either an ex-founder member, or the museum's original ticket lady still waiting for her pension.

Reaching Fateh Sagar Lake, we took a small boat over to the Nehru Park, a beautifully landscaped garden island full of bright maroon, orange and green flowers and foliage. The small restaurant here served only ice-creams and drinks. We had a lot of difficulty with the ice-creams. A flock of hungry sparrows settled all around us waiting for leftovers. It was just like a scene out of *The Birds*.

Our final call, the Jagdish Temple, was too much for Jenny. The heat finally overpowered her, and she lay panting at the bottom, unable to get up the steps. I climbed up alone and found a group of Rajasthani women – dressed in traditional bright, flowing robes – seated within the cool interior, singing religious songs. They were accompanied by a skilled tabla-drum player, and the songs were both tuneful and atmospheric. Shortly after I had sat down to listen, a doddering old man dressed in a little white dhoti appeared and began performing a shuffling dance to the music. His hands moved to and fro restlessly as he tottered about, suggesting the spirited motion his feet would have liked to achieve had they not been so unsteady. Suddenly, the song changed and the women launched into an altogether more frenetic number. At which point, the old dotard stopped in mid-shuffle, and shambled slowly off the floor looking affronted.

After handing in my shoes at the entrance, I was compelled to view the temple itself at high speed, for the ground was now white-hot from the sun and sizzled the soles of my feet whenever I paused to look at anything.

Having returned to the Rang Niwas, I tucked into a huge plate of grapes, apples, bananas, mangos, *chikus* (a bit like dates) and mandarin orange segments, while chatting to one of the hotel's owners. This was a young fresh-faced Hindu called Bahti. He had a wistful, resigned expression, particularly when talking about women and sex. Twenty-two years old, he was unhappy that caste and religious restrictions made it impossible for him to make friends with the opposite sex. The first woman he would know on an intimate basis, he confided, would be the wife 'chosen' for him by his mother. He had seen the woman to whom he was betrothed only twice to date, and disliked her intensely. I asked Bahti when his marriage would take place. 'Oh, I don't know,' he sighed dismally. 'My mother will take care of that. I'll be the very last person to know.'

Finishing our supper at the air-conditioned Berry's Restaurant in Chetak Circle, we emerged into the dark street and saw a large sign saying: 'English and Udaipur Wines'. Fancy finding a *wine* shop in India, we thought, and approached it eagerly to make a purchase. I gave the proprietor an expectant smile, and asked to see his selection of wines. He looked up and replied: 'Wine? Oh, I am sorry, but we do not have any wine just at present.'

'No wine?' I echoed flatly, then insisted: 'But you're a *wine* shop – it says so on your sign!' The man gave me an apologetic look. 'Yes, sir,' he replied. 'We are most certainly a wine shop. But we are not selling wine. Here, when people ask for wine, they are thinking of buying whisky or rum. Not wine.'

April 17th

After gorging ourselves on mangos, we moved out by bicycle in search of the infamous Pratap Country Inn, a hotel with such a bad reputation that it simply begged a visit. According to Bahti, it was run by a middle-aged relative of his who lured susceptible western women into his lecherous embraces by giving them free dips in his mud-hole swimming pool and free horse-riding lessons in his ramshackle stables afterwards.

We set out at 10.30am. By noon, we were hopelessly lost. And my bicycle had developed a flat back tyre. I left it in a repair shop we found in the middle of nowhere, and sat down with Jenny in the shade over a cup of tea. The bicycle-repair man came over to give me an offer I couldn't refuse: the bike needed a new valve fitted and this would cost me twenty rupees. He had made sure I couldn't refuse by removing the old valve, making an inexpensive temporary repair impossible. Piqued, I told him I couldn't afford the new valve, and wobbled off again with the flat tyre.

We never reached the Pratap Country Inn. Somehow, we ended up at the Maharajah of Udaipur's hunting lodge at the Hotel Shikarbadi. The only life we had seen for miles was a pondful of static water-buffalo. As we passed up to the hotel, however, a host of large white monkeys with wise, black faces darted out to greet us. So did the hotel's strange doorman, an elderly Indian who rushed towards us in a flowing scarlet dress-coat, flourishing a long, deadly scimitar. He dismissed our show of alarm, and directed us to the restaurant for drinks. Relaxing here in cool, shaded green wicker chairs, we asked the waiter if we could possibly use the hotel's swimming pool, for the heat had dried us to a crisp. He said he didn't know, but would find out from the manger. The manager's office was just round the corner, but the waiter probably decided the walk was too arduous. He preferred to use the telephone. It took him twenty minutes to get through. He spoke to the manager, and then returned to tell us that yes, we could use the pool, but it would cost us twenty rupees each. A short, hurried consultation, followed by a pooling of resources, and we agreed to pay the required fee.

The Shikarbadi had an excellent swimming pool. It had luxury tiling, was ideally positioned to catch the best of the sun, and was surrounded by reclining couches in which to get the perfect tan. The only thing it didn't have, however, was water. We reached the edge of the pool to find it quite empty.

Somehow, despite the bicycle's flat tyre, I negotiated the five kilometres back to Udaipur without incident. And there were some charming sights along the way, particularly of the brightly-attired Rajasthani women – their robes of yellow, green, red and orange billowing behind them as they passed by (often singing) with panniers of food or bales of hay balanced on their heads. Later, we saw an overheated elephant with a load of pots and pans on its back, standing in a ditch, cooling off in the shade of some trees with its sleeping master. Not so lucky was the heat-maddened bull which ran amok down the street as we approached the City Palace. It was so crazed, it nearly butted Jenny off her bicycle.

Back at the Roof Garden Cafe, 'God' turned up again. His urbane veneer of sophistication was slipping tonight. He confessed that for all his money, his good job and house, and his rich friends, he felt something lacking. He didn't know what. To stop himself thinking about it, he asked the waiter to put on his favourite record. It was a mournful soul number which, when slurred out of the restaurant's decrepit tape machine, crept long at a funereal pace. It opened with the ominous statement: 'This...is...the...saddest...day...of...my...life', and it depressed us enormously.

But Dev loved it. He said it put him in mind of a beautiful woman he had once loved who had spurned him for someone with more money. And again, he gave Jenny his undivided attention all evening.

April 18th

We only just caught the early bus out to Chittorgarh this morning. One second, the driver was leisurely consuming a sticky *jellaby* (sweetmeat) and sipping a cup of tea; the next, he had leapt into his small cockpit and roared the bus out of the stand. Which was rather unfortunate for Jenny, who had just sauntered off to buy us some breakfast. By the time she returned a minute later, carefully carrying two cups of cha and a bunch of bananas, the bus-rank was empty. She looked thunderstruck. It was only with difficulty that I persuaded the impetuous driver to reverse back up and collect her.

But the whole of the rest of the journey went like this. No sooner had the bus stopped, than the driver was off out of his seat to get his cup of tea, and we didn't see hide or hair of him until, when we least expected it, he was magically back in his seat and raring to go again. It was a nerve-racking experience. The first couple of stops, we disembarked to get some tea ourselves, but no sooner had we queued up and purchased it than the driver had rematerialised in the bus, his teeth bared in a manic grin, and we had to abandon our drinks untouched and race back to the bus again before it skidded off without us.

Apart from that, the four-and-a-half hour journey was smooth and pleasant. We came into Chittorgarh relaxed, and with our plan of action ready. We had just two hours spare before our next bus left at 3pm for Ajmer. Moving into high gear we hired a rickshaw and told the driver to take us round Chittor's main attractions as quickly as possible.

Chittorgarh is a massive fortified city with a very famous history. In olden days, whenever it was attacked and saw its position hopeless, all the men would ride out to be slaughtered in one last glorious battle while all the women and children committed suicide. Each time this happened – and there had been three such 'Jauhars' of note – almost the entire population of the city had been wiped out. The miracle was that it managed to restock itself each time to ready for the *next* mass suicide.

Our lightning tour took us up through Chittor's seven forti-fied gates, into the modern Fateh Prakash Palace, and then up to the top of the impressive Tower of Victory, with a magnifi-cent view of the whole fort ruins. We then passed round the Mahasati site – a sad, lonely place where many brave wives and concubines joined their husbands on the funeral pyres – and finished up at the lovely Padmini Palace, set in calm, tran-quil courtyards and gardens. It was on the pavilion of this pal-ace, so the story goes, that the beautiful princess Padmini stood when the emperor Alu-ud-Din saw her reflection in a mirror and fell in love. He was so infatuated that he destroyed the whole of Chittor to get her. In the end, Padmini decided to cheat him of his prize by killing herself – yet another example of this unhappy people's remarkable talent for self-destruction.

Leaving Chittorgarh, we came to Ajmer, and caught the short connecting bus to Pushkar, arriving there shortly after dusk. A small oasis of civilisation located on the edge of the Great Thar Desert, this town had been recommended to us by many other travellers as the most pleasant place to stay in all India.

April 19th

From the parapets of the cheap but palatial Pushkar Hotel, I noted this morning that we were staying on the banks of a small inland lake. There was a fine view of the whole town, the small houses and shops glittering marble-white in the re-flected light of the rising sign.

Coming down for breakfast, I met Paul, a friend from Ko-dai, who advised us to seek out the Krishna Restaurant, apparently the best place for food in town. It took us a long time to reach it, however. There were too many distractions. The quiet, friendly streets of Pushkar are absolutely crammed with attractive, colourful shops selling all manner of marvellous clothes, shoes, curios, souvenirs, tapestries, and wall-hangings. With the possible exception of Kathmandu, it is the very best place to meet interesting people and to buy interesting things – though the very worst place to go if one is a poor traveller living on a very tight budget. There is far too much tempting stuff to buy here, and it's all far too cheap to resist.

By the time we reached Krishna's for breakfast, it was lunch-time. Within, I discovered my old trekking companion, Joseph, sitting in a corner with a bag of guava pears. It was a very happy reunion, enlivened by the Krishna's interesting menu. This offered PLAIN SLUICE, MACRONY CHEESE, VEGE SENDVICH and JEM TOST ONE PLATE. It also bore the stern warning: SUGGAR CHAGGE WILL BE EXTRA! The Krishna also had a speaking fridge. It stood in the corner and was plastered with stickers saying things like: WELCOME! and DON'T TOUCH ME! and I AM VERY COLD! It was a real conversation piece.

After a delicious fruit salad curd, followed by a curious porridge made from chapti wheat, I suggested that Jenny have her hair cut. It was getting too long for comfort in this heat. But the Indian barber we found didn't understand English too well. Instead of cutting just one inch off, as she had requested, he left just one inch *on.* She now had as much hair as me – i.e. hardly any. But the result suited her well. And as her flowing auburn locks fell to the floor, Megan turned up. She had left the other Scottish girls behind in Jaipur, and had travelled over to join us here in Pushkar.

The heat of the day had now reached fireball intensity. To

finance further shopping expeditions, I now sold my Walkman and we returned – part of the way on camel-back – to move all our bags over to the Sarovar Tourist Bungalow, where Joseph was staying. This turned out be the most luxurious (and least expensive) lodgings I had taken in India. My room was a tiny one – in an octagonal castle turret – but the rest of the building, and its facilities, were unsurpassed. Festoons of green plants, gardens of bright-hued trees, lawns of lush grass, beautiful views of the lake, and the awesome mountain backdrop made this the perfect spot in Pushkar in which to wind down and relax. After a few hours of basking in the sun and swimming in the lake's calm, warm waters, we gave this place our vote for the nearest thing to paradise we'd found in all India.

We only exerted ourselves once more today – to steer Megan off to the barbers to get her hair cut too. She also emerged practically bald. Otherwise, all we found to do in Pushkar was swim, sunbathe, go shopping, and drink ice-cold Limcas and lemon sodas.

April 20th

Before it became too hot, we took an early morning trek across the rolling dunes of the desert and up to a nearby hilltop temple.

Once out of Pushkar town, the desert sands stretched before us into infinity. We crossed them in silence and came half an hour later to the foot of a giant stone causeway, some thousand feet high, which led up to the temple. Reaching the top – a hot, sweaty climb – we entered the tiny shrine to find a refreshing cup of mint tea waiting for us. It was served by an Australian girl who, dressed in native garb and fluent in Hindi, was being allowed to attend the temple. She told us that it was some two thousand years old, and had been erected in honour of the god Brahma's first wife, Savitri.

The views were quite superb. Below us, Pushkar and its lake glistened like a bright blue tear in the eye of the surrounding desert. Barren plains and mountains lay north and south of the town, while to the rear a speck-size mule train was ambling off into miles upon miles of arid, undulating sands. We spent an hour here, then returned back down before the sun became too intense for walking.

Going back into town, we stopped off at the pink-domed Brahma Temple, apparently the only temple in all India built specifically for the god Brahma. Which we found odd, since Brahma is the central figure (Creator) in Indian mythology. The temple itself was the cleanest, quietest and most attractive we had ever come across. And all the local people paying their devotions here were extremely welcoming.

The rest of the day was spent in spending too much money. Everywhere we walked, our pockets emptied to purchase embroidered waistcoats, silk trousers, mirror-inlaid bags and all manner of baubles, bangles and beads. Our final expense of the day, however, was the most interesting – having our photograph taken by a grizzled old Indian owning an antique Victorian box-camera. It took a whole hour for him to set up his equipment and to produce a satisfactory negative. As we waited, sitting on a low bench at the roadside, our gaze shifted between the two donkeys that had begun to copulate in the middle of the street and the small girl with eight toes on her left foot who had come to supervise proceedings. The photo, when it was finally produced, was remarkable. It had the tinted, vignetted look of a picture taken last century!

Pushkar struck us at the cleanest, most relaxed place in India any of us had yet visited. It wasn't noisy, overpopulated, stressful or anything like as dirty as most other towns or cities. The only hubbub came from the odd pack of wild dogs, the occasional shriek of a peacock and the wild chattering of temple moneys. As for the human population, they were generally sound asleep.

April 21st

Before paying our farewells to Pushkar, we made a short tour of the holy ghats lining the banks of the lake. These were charming places, with a relaxed and friendly approach to visiting tourists. Only one ghat gave us problems: the girls were instructed to make *puja* (devotion) to the god of the lake. They were seated on the steps of the ghat, with their feet immersed in the water, and their cupped hands were filled with flower petals, rice and coloured powder. After casting this offering into the water, they were given a dried husk of coconut each to recite the 'Brahma Puja' over. This prayer, which the priests expected Megan and Jenny to repeat parrot-fashion after them had a brain-washing begging routine built into it. Thus, in between various regular prayers to Brahma, there would appear the curious instruction: 'You-give-me-twenty-one-rupees-one-hundred-and-one-rupees-no-matter-what-you-give.' When the girls only gave the priests the time of day and no rupees at all, there were angry scowls and muttered curses all round. Even here in Pushkar, we were saddened to note, religion and money went very much hand in hand.

We went down the high street towards the Krishna Restaurant through a barrage of friendly one-liners from local people. None of these passing comments – which ranged from old favourites like 'Good rate dollars' and 'You are coming from? to new curiosities like 'First time Pushkar?' and 'Fruit Porridge' – seemed to require any reply. People made them, then went on their way. Rajiv, the affable manager of the Krishna, had a lot more to say for himself. He was a 25-year old Brahmin, very concerned about his ever getting married. Not only could he not afford to keep a wife and her entire family in his house, but even if he had one, he would hardly get to see her since he had to work 14 hours a day to look after the restaurant. All this, however, was not the main problem. The main problem was that he had an elder brother. And his caste required that all the children in a family marry 'in sequence' – eldest first. The only way that a younger sibling could jump the queue was when elder brothers and sisters had mental or physical infirmities which made their own marriage unlikely. Rajiv's elder brother, however, was in perfect health. And he had no intention of getting married. Which meant that Rajiv could expect to remain a bachelor for many years, perhaps the rest of his life.

The moment we left Pushkar, our troubles started. Out of this oasis paradise, we were quickly thrown back into 'real India' again. Even getting out of the hotel was a problem. I deducted ten rupees from my bill in respect of the dhobi-wallah having dyed all my clothes purple, but the manager became awkward and had his entire staff bar the door to my exit. Rather than return home a cripple, I paid the ten rupees.

A pleasant roof-top journey on the bus back to Ajmer was followed by an arduous two hours touring round every photographic shop trying to get a sensible price for my camera. I was now low again on funds, and had to sell it. The camera eventually went for Rs800 (£20) but by this time it was far too late make Agra tonight. We decided to spend the night in Jaipur instead.

The road to Jaipur was littered with wrecked vehicles – battle-scarred victims of recent crashes – and our journey was repeatedly delayed as the roads were being cleared to allow us passage. Two crash scenes were particularly harrowing, with the offending driver of both smash-ups being set upon and beaten to a bloody pulp by the passengers of the other vehicles.

We booked into a troublesome lodge in Jaipur called the Hotel Golden. This tried to charge us a hundred-rupee 'deposit' (five times the room rent!) and gave us rooms in which all the door locks fell off. But this wasn't the worst of it. The hotel's main problem was cockroaches. It was absolutely crawling with them. I came back to my room this evening after a wholesome meal of *thali* to a full-scale conflict with the insect kingdom. It started when I switched on my light and noticed that the full packet of 'Coconut Crunchies' I had left on my table now contained just two biscuits. An army of ants, forming a neat black line from the wash-hand basin to the table, had eaten the rest. But they hadn't done it alone. I picked up the biscuit packet, and three giant cockroaches scuttled out. I picked up the table, and scores more dropped off the bottom of it. Before I knew it, the whole room was alive with scurrying roaches. They moved devilishly fast, and had iron-hard shells. Consequently, it took me a long hour to root them all out. Then I went over to Megan and Jenny's room to warn them against leaving any food out for insects. But they weren't interested. They had something much worse than cockroaches to worry about. A large black rat had just run out from under Megan's bed and was now roaming around in the room's squat-toilet. A *very* uneasy night followed.

April 22nd

Our only pleasant memory of Jaipur was its ice-cream, which was delicious. A traveller over breakfast told us we should have been here during the 'marriage season' recently, for then the city was far more colourful and friendly. He told us that every Indian in town had rushed to get married this spring after hearing that it was an astrologically auspicious time. Every marriage had been celebrated by a big procession down the high streets. The contrast between rich and poor marriages, our friend told us, was very marked. Wedding processions for the rich had plush carriages, white horses, and guests following on, holding neon-lit tubes. The poor, however, had no such finery. All they had was a tractor. And an auto-rickshaw. The rickshaw went on ahead, with a few streamers flying from it, while the guests and the gifts chugged up the road behind it on an old tractor.

Taking the bus on to Agra, I found myself sharing a seat with a portly Indian in white Congress Party dress. He was an incurable fidget. He had a bag at his feet with a Russian-made toy truck which he was itching to play with. Every minute or so, his hands would dip helplessly into the bag to spin the truck's wheels or to stroke its glossy paint.

Agra was again a scene of much hassle from rickshaw drivers, beggars and unemployed Indians wanting to change our dollars or to earn commissions by guiding us to cheap lodgings. Wishing to see the Taj Mahal unhampered by luggage, we left all our bags in a single cheap hotel room. The owner of this lodge insisted that I take a look at his 'garden', saying it would be of great interest to me. It turned out to be a small field at the back of the lodge, packed to capacity with cannabis plants.

Taking rickshaws to the Taj, we dropped off at Joney's Place, a restaurant much recommended by travellers. It is owned by a happy young Indian (Joney) who combines a real interest in Westerners with service of very fine food. After welcoming us to his establishment, he asked us to sign his 'guest book' which was full of tributes (often humorous) from satisfied customers, and then he gave us his YUM YUM MEENU. This contained a 'big breakfast' of PORICLG and CORNFX, ONE POID EGG, and YOGURT PANKAGE. Joney was particularly keen that we try his STAFFED POT (stuffed potatoes) and VEG BOMB (?). So we did. They were excellent.

We came into the Taj by the quiet South Gate. By the entrance, a small Limca stand was advertising its wares: 'LOOK HERE', said its sign. 'MAY I EXCUSE YOU FOR VERY ICE-COLD DRINK OF FREEZ?'

My second tour round the Taj Mahal was altogether more satisfying that the first. Primarily because the intense heat was now on the decline, and the blinding-white light playing on the marble monument had been replaced by a warm, orange-cream glow which rested very easy on the eye. Seated on the green lawns, we again marvelled at the ageless quality of this structure. It hardly seemed the work of human hands. Which is probably what its architect, the cruel Shah Jahan wanted people to think and why he (apparently) had the hands chopped off all the principal sculptors, lest they duplicated their remarkable achievement.

We were so taken with the Taj that we hopped on the 6.45pm train back to New Delhi only just before it pulled out of the station. This was the famous 'Taj Express' – the nearest thing to luxury travel for ordinary passengers that India can provide. Not only was there no crowding and lots of room but it was very well air-conditioned and very clean. Best of all, in view of the aching calluses on our backsides, it had well-padded seats. There was even a drinks service available – a man moving up and down the train selling ice-cold bottles of some fizzy drink called 'Tingler'.

Back in Delhi at 10pm, we returned to the Hotel Queen. Only to find it half demolished! It was in the process of being radically 'redecorated'. We had to share the one room left vacant between the three of us. And as we moved in, the hammers and mallets went back to work outside. Would our room be still standing when we woke in the morning? Or would it be just a heap of rubble like the others, with us buried under it?

April 23rd

Most of this day was spent queuing up for cinema tickets. Delhi was going wild about the arrival of *Shiva Ka Insaaf*, India's first 3-D movie, and we decided to see what all the fuss was about. It was a fateful decision. The size of the seething ticket queue outside the Sheila cinema was formidable. And the ticket window was regularly infiltrated by people who could not be bothered to queue up, or by touts buying blocks of tickets to sell on the streets at inflated prices. Every so often a policeman would appear with a heavy *lathi* club to drive these interlopers off, but even when beaten soundly over the head they got up smiling and began pushing in again.

I got in at the back of the queue at 10am. By the time I had reached the front, it was noon. And just as I was about to hand my money through the forest of other hands pressed in the ticket window, it mysteriously closed 'for lunch'. Poor Megan, sizzling away on the white-hot pavements, nearly burst into tears at this point. To retrieve the situation, I tracked down the cinema manager and he promised to have three tickets waiting for us at 3pm.So we went away and came back again at 3pm, and asked for our tickets. But they weren't there. The manger had forgotten. I ground my teeth, and prepared to rejoin the milling scrum of people 'queuing' round the ticket window. Suddenly, the situation was saved. A helpful Indian, seeing our predicament, jumped the entire queue for us and procured us three tickets. He did it simply out of the kindness of his heart. And he did it in two minutes flat.

The last event of the day was a musical entertainment outside the Metropolis Restaurant. A tabla-drum player, accompanied by a flautist and squeezebox player, was hammering out a frenetic, hypnotic rhythm in the road, with members of the large, pressing audience being invited to dance to the beat. One local boy promptly did such a good impersonation of a whirling dervish that some appreciative observer stuck a filthy two-rupee note in his open mouth. The clean-cut youth didn't like this at all. He stopped dancing, spat the money out, wiped his mouth, and strode off looking mortified.

April 24th

Queuing up to see *Shiva Ka Insaaf* outside the cinema, all eyes were fixed on Jenny and Megan. They were the only women in the queue. But as we filed up to the entrance, attention quickly switched from them to something far more interesting – a determined assault on the entrance door by hordes of Indians trying to get in without tickets. They dashed up the steps, got clubbed down again by a flurry of flashing *lathis*, scraped themselves bleeding off the ground, and dived straight back in again. The cinema manager, dispensing 3-D spectacles at the door, surveyed this with growing excitement. At last, no longer able to contain himself, he vaulted over the ticket barrier, snatched one of the *lathis* out of a policeman's hands, and waded into the crowd of illegal entrants, cracking as many heads as possible before reluctantly returning to his post.

The film itself was gloriously bizarre. It featured a meek, mild-mannered and incredibly obsequious Hindi youth who kept changing into a super-hero called 'Shiva'. Shiva was very fat and wore a kinky leather outfit, compete with black mask, flowing black cape and pointy-toed black booties. He had gained his incredible Shiva-powers (overtaking villainous Chevrolets on a Shiva-bicycle, head-butting gymnasium punch-bags for hours on end without apparent brain damage, and leaping over a swimming pool full of floating logs for a big helping of Shiva-samosas) by praying at a Muslim mosque, a Catholic church and a Hindu temple. Oh, and by dedicating himself to falling off high buildings for worthy causes.

Whenever the portly hero arrived, the film soundtrack erupted in a triumphant blare of noise, and a whispered chant of '*shiva!...Shiva!...SHIVA!*' built up to a bellowed boom in the background. This was just in case the audience hadn't guessed who was coming. When not dressed in leather and prancing around doing good deeds, Shiva was a feeble news reporter cowering under the petulant criticism and cross intolerance of the 'heroine', his editor. All she had to recommend her (as far as we could see) was a pretty good singing voice. Which meant that the otherwise omniscient Shiva was completely blind to her other failings. Like all other Indian film heroes he was a hopeless sucker for a good song.

The film as a whole, despite tidal waves of charging, militant music announcing every dramatic 3-D effect, was hugely enjoyable. It put us in just the right mood to enjoy our other main event of the day – visiting a luxury swimming pool in one of Delhi's plush hotels. This was something I had been looking forward to for months, having heard that for a reasonable charge poor tourists like ourselves could avail themselves of the very best hotel facilities that India could provide.

Our first choice, the Imperial Hotel in Janpath, was too expensive. But then we came to the nearby Hotel Kanishka, which charged only Rs25 each for use of its luxury pool and associated mod cons. We spent a marvellous afternoon there, lying on sun-beds, swimming, and having drinks brought out to us by the pool. It gave us a glimpse of how the rich tourist in India can expect to live.

Leaving the restful, enclosed haven of the hotel, however, it was back to real India again. We found ourselves stranded at the wrong end of town, every rickshaw and taxi in Delhi having decided to go on strike while we lazed obliviously by the pool. It took us a long hour trampling round the city to find just one young rickshaw 'blackleg' who would defy the strike to take us home.

I packed and made ready to leave India. Then, with the approach of evening, I took the girls down to Gobind's for a farewell meal. It was a small affair of fruit salad and curd, with lemon tea, taken on the upstairs balcony. From here, I took my last look at Indian life passing by on the streets below. It was the same as usual: a busy, chaotic, yet strangely harmonious potpourri of noise, colour and smells. Beggars huddled in doorways, children cried and laughed and ran wild, rickshaws bleeped and hooted and ploughed onwards relentlessly, sacred cows lay unconcerned in the middle of the road, and tourists picked their way carefully round the excrement and the gaping open sewers on the pavements. It almost seemed ordinary now.

Two events alone remained in my memory long after this last view of Delhi had passed. The first was when an angry old Sikh nabbed two young thieves in the act of robbing the till of his restaurant next door. Both of the youths were also Sikhs, but this didn't stop the old man whacking them round the head with a large club. It also didn't stop the typical curious crowd of onlookers gathering from miles around to watch. But were the young reprobates repentant of their crime? None of it. They just rubbed their cracked heads and grinned and giggled like naughty children who enjoyed the attention and who would doubtless repeat the offence at the earliest possible opportunity. Even when a couple of passing policemen on a motorbike chopped them down with well-aimed *lathi* blows to the back of the knees, they showed no remorse, but simply got up and strolled off laughing.

And the second was the sight of a dazed young Westerner staggering down the street below us. Like many long-stay backpackers in India, he had sustained an injury, and wore a dirty bandage round his wrist. He was also doped up to his eyeballs. So much so indeed, that he had no control over his movements and simply tottered up and down the dark road bumping into Indian pedestrians.

My final trip with the girls was to the Connaught Place bus-rank, which ran a late-night service to Delhi airport. Somehow, all three of us (together with my luggage) managed to squeeze into a single cycle-rickshaw. The ride was remarkable in that it restored my faith in Indian rickshaw drivers. The young cyclist made no complaints the whole way, despite his very heavy load. He made no demands for black-market business, just smiled and got on with his job. I was so impressed with him that when he asked me for two rupees at the bus-rank, I gave him ten. Caught completely by surprise as this vast sum (actually less than £1), he gave the note a big kiss and beamed us a smile of eternal gratitude.

I paid my farewells to Megan and Jenny over a cup of coffee in the quiet Palace Restaurant, near the bus-rank. We were the last three guests of the day, and the waiters hovered around us anxiously, waiting for us to leave and let them go to bed. This last restaurant I visited in India, somewhat appropriately, turned out to have the most deliciously mis-spelt menu – including mouth-watering specialities like CHICKEN MARRY LAND, CHICKEN STRONGOFF, BRAIN CURRY, BOMBOO SHOOT and CHICKEN GOBLET. The 'piece de resistance', to our mind, was however a Chinese dish called FRIED WANTON. And not only could you have your 'wanton' fried, but any which way you wanted her – including WANTON, VEG OR NON-VEG, or WANTON, ONE PLATE, or even WANTON AND CHIPS!

~ THE END ~

Postscript

Off the plane back in Heathrow, I did not – unlike Kevin – have a plateful of cheese sandwiches waiting for me in the airport lounge. I returned straight home and ate a simple meal of rice and yoghurt – the nearest thing to an Indian *thali* I could find.

Then I ran a bath, my first in four months, and discovered on the scales that I was two whole stones lighter than when I had left England. Finally, I climbed into bed, faintly aware of the deafening silence in the streets outside, and slept for a whole day.

I woke up feeling like I had been rung through a mangle backwards. Then, as consciousness returned, I found myself thinking of my next journey.

Where would I be going?

Why, back to India of course!

Hi folks, Frank here!

Thank you so much for reading my book, I do hope you enjoyed it! If you did, I would be extremely grateful if you could leave a few words on Amazon as a review: http://authl.it/274 Not only are reviews crucial in getting an author's work noticed, but I personally love reviews and treasure them all…even the slightly stinky ones!

Oh, and if you *really* enjoyed this book, then maybe you'd like the two sequels, 'Off the Beaten Track: My Crazy Year in Asia' http://authl.it/21z and 'Rupee Millionaires' http://authl.it/vy They're more of my madcap adventures in Asia!

P.S. If you like, you can find me on Twitter:
https://twitter.com/Wussyboy

Or catch me on Facebook:
https://www.facebook.com/frank.kusy.5?ref=tn_tnmn

Or if you get the urge, you can always email me:
sparky-frank@hotmail.co.uk

Acknowledgements

I would like to thank Kevin Bloice (did we really do all that half a lifetime ago?), to Anna Donovan (for my lovely cover), to Cherry Gregory (for the final beta read), and to Jean-Luc Barbanneau (for publishing the first editions of 'Kevin and I' and for giving his kind permission for this one).

A special thanks goes to Roman Laskowski for his meticulous editing and formatting. Top job, mate!

𝒻rank 𝒦usy

About the Author

FRANK KUSY is a professional travel writer with nearly thirty years experience in the field. He has written guides to India, Thailand, Burma, Malaysia, Singapore and Indonesia. Of his first work, the travelogue *Kevin and I in India* (1986), the Mail on Sunday wrote: 'This book rings so true of India that most of us will be glad we don't have to go there.'

Born in England (of Polish-Hungarian parents), Frank left Cardiff University for a career in journalism and worked for a while at the Financial Times. India is his first love, the only country he knows which improves on repeated viewings. He still visits for business and for pleasure at least once a year. He lives in Surrey, England, with his wife Margreet and his little cat Sparky.

GRINNING BANDIT BOOKS

A word from our sponsors…

If you enjoyed *Kevin and I in India*, please check out these other brilliant books:

Rupee Millionaires, Off the Beaten Track: My Crazy Year in Asia, Ginger the Gangster Cat, Ginger the Buddha Cat – all by Frank Kusy (Grinning Bandit Books).

Weekend in Weighton by Terry Murphy (Grinning Bandit Books).

Scrapyard Blues and *The Albion* – both by Derryl Flynn (Grinning Bandit Books).

The Ultimate Inferior Beings by Mark Roman (Cogwheel Press).

16049567R00141

Printed in Great Britain
by Amazon